val de bagnes

second edition 2004

written and edited by
Isobel Rostron & Michael Kayson

Qanuk Publishing & Design Ltd
www.snowmole.com

the snowmole guide to **verbier val de bagnes**
first published in the UK in 2003 by winter press

ISBN 0-9545739-0-0

the snowmole guide to **verbier val de bagnes**
second edition 2004

published by Qanuk Publishing & Design Ltd
45 Mysore Road London SW11 5RY

printed by Craftprint, Singapore

ISBN 0-9545739-2-7

A catalogue record of this book is available from the British Library.

snowmole does not accept any advertising or payment, and the guides are written free from any bias.

The contents of this book are believed correct at the time of printing. As things can change, errors or omissions may occur. The publishers and authors can accept no responsibility for any loss, injury or inconvenience sustained by anybody using information or comment contained in this guide.

contents

how to use the guide

How much you enjoy your winter holiday depends on a variety of things. Some you cannot influence - you can't guarantee sunshine, good snow, or your flight landing on time... but most things should be within your control. With the majority of ski holidays lasting just a week or less, you don't want to waste time trying to find a good restaurant, or struggling with an overgrown piste map. The snowmole guides are designed with 2 purposes in mind: to save you time by providing essential information on the operation of the resort, and to help you to make the most of your time by giving insight into every aspect of your stay.

The guide is not intended to be read from cover to cover. After the introduction to the resort, the guide is split into 4 distinct sections - getting started, the skiing, the resort and the a-z - so you can dip into the information you need when you need it. Some information will be useful to you beforehand, some while you are in resort and some while you are on the mountain.

getting started deals with the basics: how to get to the resort, how to get around once you're there, and your options when buying your lift pass, renting equipment and booking lessons or mountain guides.

the skiing gives an overview of the mountains and the ski area, information on the off-piste, and a breakdown for beginners, intermediates, experts, boarders and non-skiers. The ski domain has been divided into digestible chunks and for each there is a detailed description of the pistes and lifts.

the resort covers the best of the rest of your holiday: a series of reviews on where to eat, where to play, what to do when skiing isn't an option, facilities for children and tips for seasonnaires. Those places that deserve a lengthier review are written as a 'feature'.

the a-z comprises a list of tour operators, a directory of contact details (telephone numbers and website addresses) and information from accidents to weather, a glossary of terms used in this guide and in skiing in general, and an index to help navigate your way around the guide.

how to use the maps

The guide also features a number of maps, designed and produced specifically for snowmole. While the information they contain is as accurate as possible, some omissions have been made for the sake of clarity.

route maps show the journey to the resort from the UK, from relevant airports or the roads within the area surrounding the resort.

resort maps for the resort as a whole (showing pedestrianised zones, car parks, main buildings, train lines, and road names) and individual maps showing by type the places we review.

ski maps each individual area has its own contoured map. These show details such as the lifts, pistes and mountain restaurants. The contours have been mapped to fit an A6 page - few ski areas are perfect rectangles. They are accurate only in relation to the pistes they depict and should not be used for navigation. Pistes are shown only in their approximate path - to make the maps as user-friendly as possible some twists and turns have been omitted. The ski maps are grouped together at the back of the book to make them easy to find and refer to - even with gloves on. There is an overview map on the inside back cover that shows the entire ski domain and how the individual ski maps fit together. The back cover has a flap, which is useful as a page marker for the individual ski maps. In the chapter on the skiing the overview map is reproduced in miniature alongside the descriptions of the individual sectors.

explanation of icons

review headers

basic details

- telephone number
- fax number
- email address
- website address
- number of beds
- office address
- opening hours
- food type

ski school icons

- ski lessons
- snowboard lessons
- child-specific lessons
- disabled skiing
- specialist courses
- G - guides available

hotel icons

- on-site rental store
- shuttle bus

others

- food available
- take away
- live music
- tv
- internet station(s)
- bar
- terrace

town maps

buildings

- tourist office
- lift pass office
- post office
- supermarket
- cinema
- church

travel specific

- P - parking
- P - covered parking
- bus stop
- route specific bus stop

commerce colour coding

- savoyarde restaurant
- restaurant
- cafe
- take-away
- bar
- nightclub
- hotel

route maps

 - train line & station

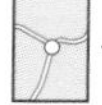 - main road & town

 - country borders

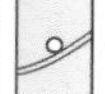 - motorway & town

 - airport

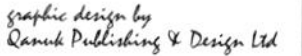

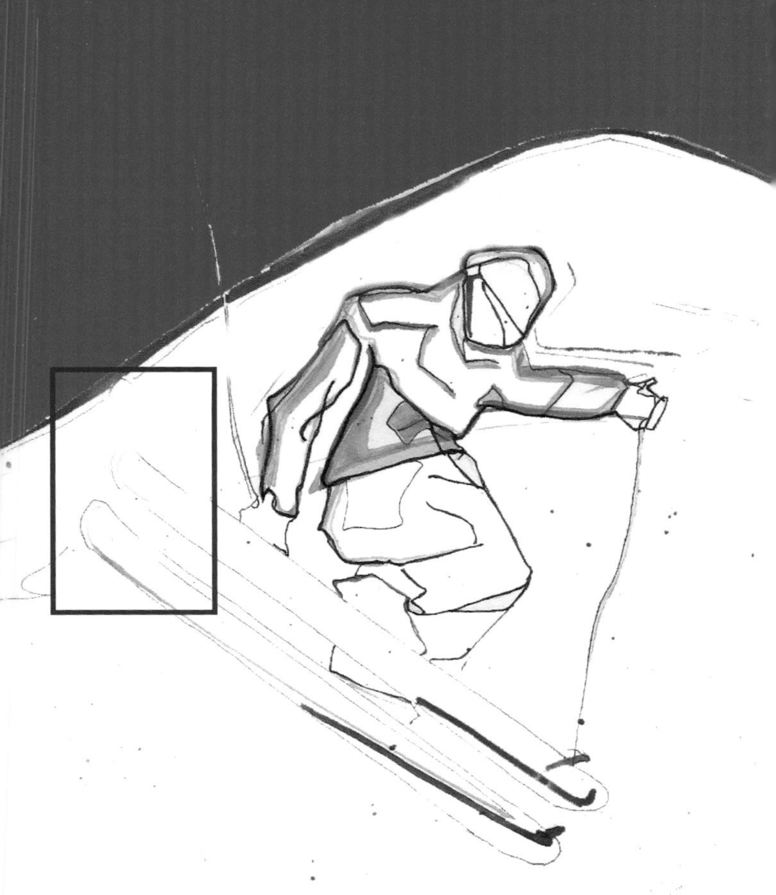

introducing verbier

overview

Verbier's rise to the top of the ski resort popularity charts has been impressive. A mere youngster compared to other well-established Swiss resorts such as Wengen and Zermatt - development only boomed in the 1960s when skiing became a recreational sport for the masses - Verbier is now internationally renowned. Such is the catalogue of its charms, it is difficult to pin down a single reason for its success - whatever you look for in a skiing holiday, Verbier will provide it. Every year more and more skiers make it their destination of choice.

What is known as Verbier is actually several small villages merged together on a south-west facing plateau, which is visible from the approach road along the valley floor. Lying between altitudes of 1400m and 1600m most of the houses are built in the chalet style so much associated with the Alps, and sprawl from as high as they dare on the avalanche-prone slopes of Savoleyres all the way across to the trees beyond Médran. There are few high-rise blocks to spoil the view, and despite Verbier's relative infancy as a resort, it doesn't feel purpose-built like the blocky resorts of Tignes or Flaine in France. The highest building is the distinctive Catholic church with its tall, white tower that dwarfs the other buildings and has a charm all of its own.

But something stops Verbier from being picture-postcard perfect - perhaps because in size the village stretches almost as far as the eye can see and is still growing, or because even when the snow falls at resort level it rarely settles for long before melting. Verbier is not car-free, and at weekends the main roads through the village can become gridlocked with day-trippers. However, the view from the village is awe-inspiring - a 360° panorama of majestic peaks including Grand Combin (4314m) and, further afield, the Mont Blanc range. Verbier has an average of 300 days of sunshine a year, so more often than not the backdrop is a blue, cloudless sky - which is hard to beat.

Over half the visitors to Verbier are Swiss, many coming from Geneva, Lausanne and other nearby towns for the weekend. The rest are a mix of English, German, Italian, Scandinavian and American. Verbier has a bit of a pashmina and pearls reputation and regularly attracts celebrities and European royalty. While there are pockets of the cash-rich in the more up-market bars and clubs and you will spot the odd fur coat teamed with Chanel boots tottering down Rue de Médran, Verbier is not as showy as places like St. Moritz and Gstaad.

For somewhere to stay the full spectrum of accommodation is available - though the bulk is found in mid-range chalets and hotels, there are enough top-end chalets and 4* (and one 5*) hotels to please those seeking luxury and even a dormitory hostel to please those seeking a bargain. Whatever kind of bed you like to lie in, it's a good idea to book well ahead.

snapshot

highs...
cosmopolitan atmosphere
extensive pisted area
excellent off-piste skiing
expansive terrain park
300 days of sunshine per year on average

and lows
one of Europe's most expensive resorts
limited skiing for beginners
overcrowded slopes in peak weeks
heavy traffic at weekends
rarely snow on the streets

Verbier's après-ski and nightlife has something for almost everybody, whether your taste is for a vin chaud in the afternoon sunshine or a turn on the dancefloor in the early hours. The always busy après scene starts on the mountain but is mainly centred along Rue de Médran, only a short walk from the end of the main ski run down to the village and perfectly manageable in ski boots.

If you plan to eat out, the resort has much to offer. The wide variety of restaurants serve expensive but generally good local or international cuisine, and for those wanting something more low-key (and lower priced) there are a few brasseries, pizzerias and cafés. The choice on the mountain is a more limited range of standard fare self-service halls and a few mountain huts.

Real skiing enthusiasts would suggest that it is the varied, demanding and apparently limitless skiing that draws people back to Verbier year after year. Verbier is the westernmost resort in Switzerland's extensive 4 Vallées ski area - nearly 100 lifts link several valleys and resorts from Thyon, Veysonnaz and Nendaz, through Siviez and La Tzoumaz to Verbier, and including the area above the hamlet of Bruson across the valley from Verbier. The pisted area has a huge 400kms of pistes of varying degrees of difficulty, making it hard for intermediate skiers to get bored in a week's holiday. There are 2 main launching points from the resort - the lift stations of Médran and Savoleyres - and while the lift system in Verbier and the 4 Vallées has a reputation for being slow, antiquated and susceptible to long queues, in recent years TéléVerbier has improved many of the lifts around Verbier, installing newer, faster links in some of the traditional blackspots. And the hands-free lift pass system at least makes it feel modern. Boarders are looked after as equally well - Verbier maintains one of the biggest snowparks in the Alps.

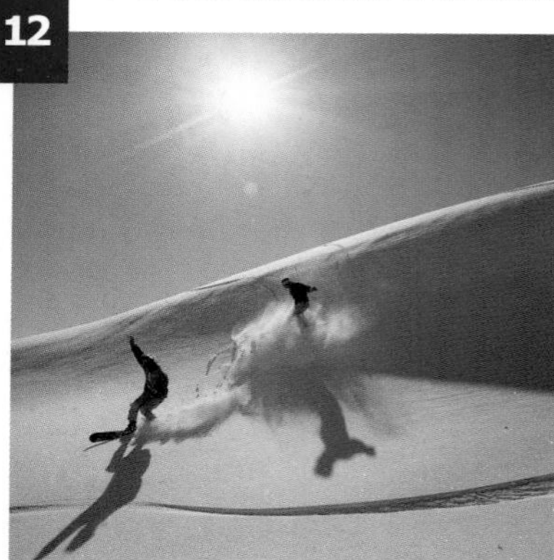

While the attraction of the pisted runs may be common knowledge, not so many are aware that Verbier has backcountry skiing to rival ski resorts across the Atlantic and closer neighbours like Chamonix. For those in the know, and with the ability, it is Verbier's numerous ungroomed descents that call them back - the unpisted area is similar in size to the pisted area. There is seemingly endless potential away from the markers, from a brief dip into the unknown to tours lasting for days at a time.

Weather in the mountains is always unpredictable, but the gods of sunshine and clement conditions seem to smile more on Verbier than on other resorts, so don't forget to pack the suncream.

temperatures

Temperatures are easy to generalise - December and January are usually the coldest months, with things warming up through February, March and April. Don't be fooled by appearances though - it is often colder when the ski is cloudless and than when snow is falling. Temperatures can range from as low as -10°C in the resort (and colder up the mountain) to as high as 20°C late on in the season when the sun is shining.

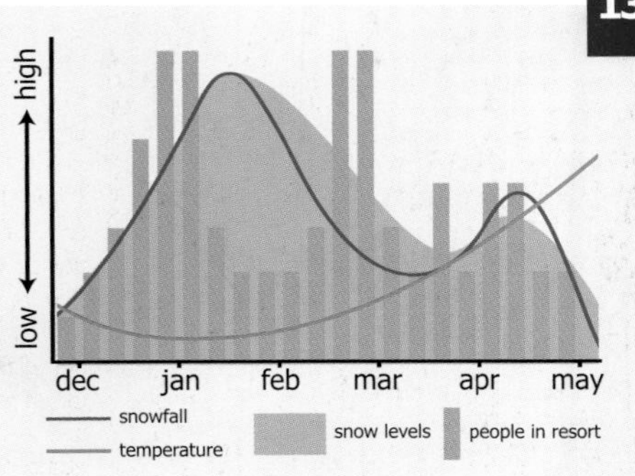

snowfall

When and how much snow falls varies from year to year, but trends do emerge. In a typical year, the first snow falls on the upper slopes in October. By Christmas, there is generally enough snow cover to make all but the very lowest slopes skiable - and even these can be opened with help from the snow cannons. The fall normally continues through January and historically the pistes have their best coverage in February. As temperatures rise, levels drop off. April can have surprising good conditions often having more snowfall than March - towards the end of the season many Verbier regulars wait eagerly for the "April dump". However, because by then it is normally warmer, what falls barely settles on the lower slopes before melting, and higher up lasts only a day or two.

volume of people in resort

Like other major resorts, Verbier's peak weeks are Christmas, New Year, the English and French school half terms (in February) and Easter, when it falls early in the year. Outside these times, special events like the Verbier Ride (➥ events & activities) make certain weekends and weeks busier than other resorts are in the same weeks. Weekends are also busy when the local Swiss flood in.

Ski resorts are as varied as DNA. But what makes Verbier Verbier? To have a quintessential time...

see stars

Hard to say which celeb put Verbier on the showbiz skiing circuit - but since Fergie was a chalet girl there in the 1980s it was bound to happen. Now it's not unusual to find yourself next to Posh and Becks in the lift queue, to race Britney for the last table at the Furry and to dance the funky chicken with another ginger but slightly younger royal in the Farm (➥ après-ski & nightlife).

have a bumpy ride

If you ski Verbier without hitting a bumpy patch you're almost missing the point. Tortin, the resort's most infamous itinerary route, is known for its mammoth moguls. And your stories about skiing the black piste from the top of Mont Fort will only be worth listening to if you can vouch for the bumps being waist-high. If either of those options sound a little too unsmooth, there's always plenty of piste-side pockmarks to get your legs warmed up - just don't forget to bend ze knees.

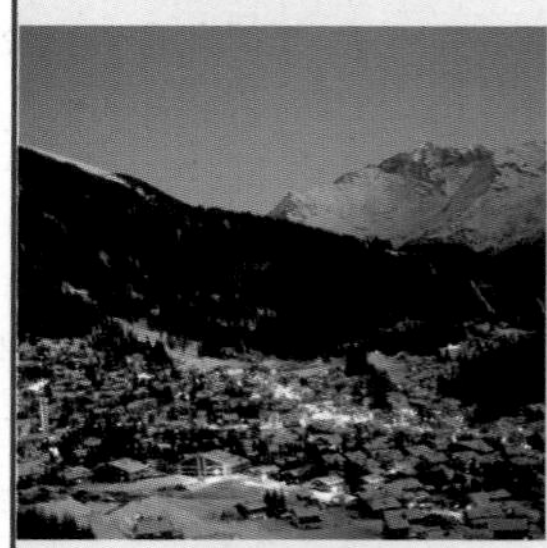

go window-shopping

Always a pleasant pastime, and one that the bakery on Rue de Verbier takes literally. Should you feel some hunger pangs while shuffling home in the early morning after shuffling the night away on the dance floor you can stop at the small window at the side of the bakery and exchange CHF2 for an oven-hot pain au chocolat.

get some bottle

Though you may need it aplenty to ski some of Verbier's more extreme slopes, here we're talking about the glass kind. Gin, vodka, rum, whisky... all of Verbier's nightclubs sell spirits by the bottle. It's quite a big one-off payment (normally CHF200) - though mixers are then thrown in for free - but if you're travelling in a big group or planning some heavy drinking it can be a good investment. And if you don't polish it off in one sitting, the friendly bar staff will label it with your name and keep it behind the bar for your next visit (whilst crossing their fingers that you don't return). So get some bottle - or depending upon how long you're staying, maybe just the one.

take a road well travelled

A visit to Verbier isn't complete without a visit to Chez Dany, a small mountain restaurant on the plateau of Clambin. Though it is someway off the pisted track and can only be reached along an ungroomed itinerary route, the path there is well-beaten and as long as you follow the ski tracks made before yours you'll soon be sipping a refreshing Cardinal in buzzy surrounds while enjoying one of Verbier's best views.

be cheesy

In your choice of food, at least. In Verbier fondues are as easy to come by as ski equipment, both on the mountain and in the town. And the aromatic Chaumière on Rue de Médran sells fabulous local dairy produce so you can even have it for breakfast, or whenever else might feel appropriate.

take a moonlit stroll

Or rather a sleigh ride. Two restaurants on the hill - Chez Dany at Clambin and Marmotte on Savoleyres - open for evening diners. As neither can be reached by car, ski-doo or feet are the only ways up. And without question a sledge is the best and most enjoyable way down. Coincide your trip with a full moon and the journey home through the moonlit forest will be unforgettable.

get lost in the woods

The forests above Bruson are both a safe(ish) place to learn the trade and a superb place to hone your tree-skiing skills. If you've never tried it before there are various routes that wind past a trunk or two and unless you have a terrible sense of direction you'll never get too far from a piste on the way down.

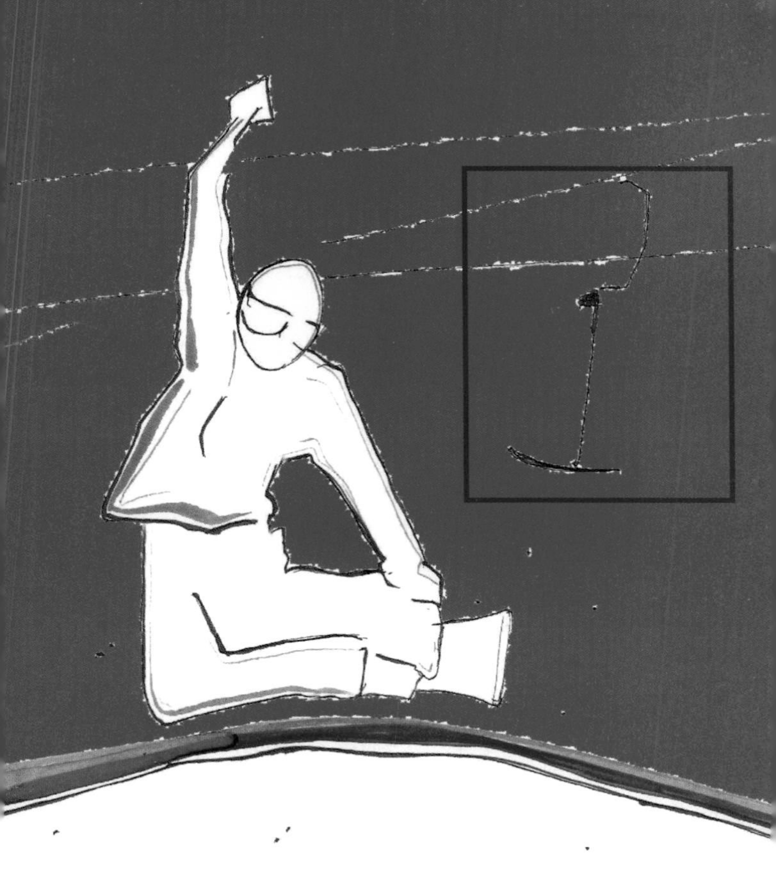

getting started

Once you know you want to go to Verbier, you need to decide how you want to get there. Traditionally, most skiing holidays are booked though travel agents or tour operators, but with the advent of cheap flights, DIY holidays are becoming more popular. There are pros and cons to both.

18 package

The theory behind package holidays is that all you should have to think about is getting from the top of the slopes to the bottom. The core of every package deal is convenience - though it comes wrapped in all kinds of paper. Ski companies fall into 2 types: large mainstream operators, and smaller more specialist ones. The mainstream brand offers ready-made holidays, where everything is already planned and you take it or leave it. Trips with smaller companies can be more expensive, but tend to be more flexible and many tailor the trip to your exact requirements. Alternatively, if you don't want to be restricted to 1 operator, a travel agent will have access to a selection of holidays offered by several companies.

Mainstream companies only run week-long trips, from Saturday to Saturday or Sunday to Sunday - giving you 6 days on the slopes and 7 nights in (or on) the town. They charter their own **flights** - making the holiday cheaper - but you have little option as to when or from where you travel. Smaller ski companies give you greater choice - many specialise in long weekends for the 'money-rich, time-poor' market, with departures on Thursday evenings and returns on Monday evenings. This gives you 4 days skiing for 2 days off work... but the real advantage is their use of scheduled flights, so you can pick the airport, airline, and when you travel.

With a mainstream company, your **transfer** to resort will be by coach, with others who have booked through the same company. You may have to wait for other flights, and on the way there may be stop-offs in other resorts or at other accommodation before your own. Because you're travelling at the weekend the journey tends to take longer. With a smaller company you may transfer by coach, minibus, taxi, or car depending on how much you've paid and the size of your group. And if you arrive mid-week, the transfers tend to be quicker.

What your **accommodation** is depends entirely on whom you book with. Different companies have deals with different hotels, some specialise in chalets, some operate in specific resorts... the limiting factor is what's in the brochure - though if you want to stay in a particular hotel, a more specialist company may try to organise it for you.

In **resort** some companies offer a drop-off and pick-up service from the lifts, which is a huge advantage in sprawling Verbier. But the main benefit of a package holiday is the resort rep. From the moment you arrive to the moment you leave, there is someone whose job it is to ensure your holiday goes smoothly... or that's the theory. More than likely your rep will sort out lift passes and equipment rental. Some will organise evening activities and be available for a short period every day to answer questions. Most are supported by an in-situ manager who deals with more serious issues. The more you pay for your holiday, the better your rep should be. The best are service-oriented French speakers... but it is difficult to recruit hard-working, intelligent, bilingual people to work for next to nothing. If you want to know what - or who - to expect, ask when you book.

DIY

If you DIY, you have more control over the kind of holiday you take and what you pay. But as you have to make all the arrangements, you'll need more time to plan the trip.

Both major (BA, Swiss) and budget airlines (bmibaby, Easyjet) schedule regular **flights** to European airports close to the Alps - for Verbier, the nearest international airport is Geneva. You can fly from all major UK airports, though the cheapest flights are normally from London, and the earlier you book the cheaper it will be. The airlines accept reservations for the upcoming winter from around June or July. Some chartered airlines such as Monarch or Thomas Cook airlines may also have a limited number of seats for sale. For **transfers** to your resort ➥ getting there. If you don't want to fly, the excellent European motorway system makes **driving** to the Alps surprisingly easy. Getting there by **train** is also an option.

On a DIY trip the choice of **accommodation** is endless - you are not restricted by brochures or company deals... however the easiest way to book a chalet or an apartment is through a company or website offering accommodation only, such as Interhome or ifyouski.com. You can liaise with the owners directly if you can find their details, but this is often difficult. For hotels you might be able to get a discount off the published price by contacting them directly ➥ accommodation.

In **resort** is perhaps where the difference between DIY and package is most noticeable. There is no rep on hand so you have to buy your own lift pass, organise your own equipment rental... but this can have its pluses: you can be sure that you get exactly the right type of pass and you can choose which rental shop you use.

Conveniently located within easy reach of 2 airports and only 40 minutes from the efficient European motorway system, Verbier is one of the most accessible resorts to reach. All contact details for the transport listed can be found in the directory.

overland

The most common starting place for any journey to the Alps by **car** is Calais. You can reach Calais from the UK by the **eurotunnel** or **ferry**. Then it is just over 550 miles (just under 900kms) from Calais to Verbier - a journey that can be done in 10 hours or less. The mustard town of Dijon is about two-thirds of the way if you want to make an overnight stop along the way.

The prettiest route from Dijon into Switzerland is through Besançon to the border crossing just before Vallorbe. If you don't have a motorway vignette (a windscreen sticker which allows you to use the Swiss motorways) you can buy one here. Once into Switzerland you rejoin the motorway system, passing by Lausanne and Montreux to the exit for Verbier at the town of Martigny. From there follow the signs through Sembrancher to Le Châble. At the roundabout in Le Châble, take the 3rd exit up the hill to Verbier. This last part of the journey is a steep ascent up a twisty, winding road. In snowy conditions, you may need to put on chains.

If you travel at the weekend or during the annual holidays expect traffic and delays along the Swiss motorways and the road up to Verbier.

There are 2 *péage* (toll) stops on the route south through France - you collect a ticket as you enter the motorway and then pay in cash or by credit card for your journey as you leave. Expect to pay around €50 in total for the péages and a vignette.

There are 2 alternatives to the standard **ferry** crossing to Calais. The first is with Norfolkline to Dunkirk - often quieter (and less prone to lorry strikes!) than the Calais services. The second is SpeedFerries.com - a new fast ferry service to Boulogne. SpeedFerries sells tickets on a similar basis to the budget airlines - the earlier you buy, the less you pay.

The classic way to reach the Alps from the UK by **train** is on the Snowtrain or the Eurostar overnight service. In theory travelling this way gives you more time in resort - 8 days instead of the usual 6. It's an excellent service if you live in London and are skiing in the 3 Vallées or the Espace Killy, but it doesn't work out so well for a skiing holiday in Verbier. Both services only stop in the Alps at Moûtiers, Aime and Bourg St. Maurice - all some distance from Verbier. There isn't a direct train service to Verbier from any of these stations, so you have to complete your

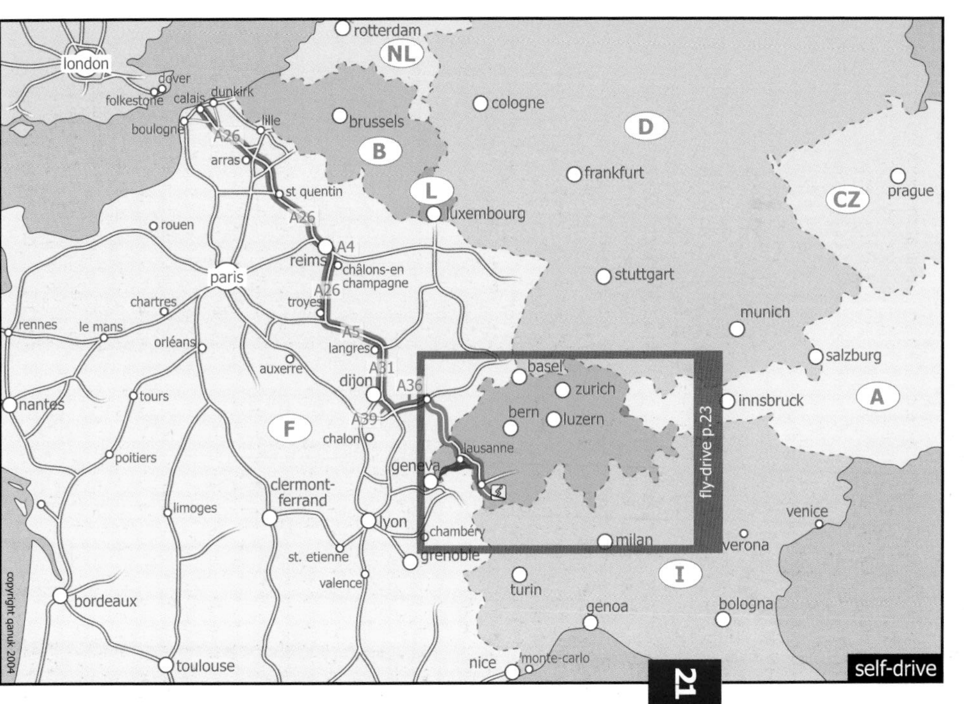
london
dover
folkestone
calais
dunkirk
boulogne
lille
A26
arras
st quentin
rotterdam
NL
brussels
B
L
luxembourg
cologne
D
frankfurt
CZ
prague
rouen
A4
reims
châlons-en
champagne
A26
paris
troyes
chartres
rennes
le mans
orléans
A5
langres
auxerre
A31
dijon
A36
A39
nantes
tours
F
chalon
poitiers
geneva
lausanne
clermont-
ferrand
limoges
lyon
chambéry
st. etienne
grenoble
valence
bordeaux
toulouse
stuttgart
munich
salzburg
basel
zurich
bern
luzern
innsbruck
A
fly-drive p.23
milan
venice
verona
I
turin
genoa
bologna
nice
monte-carlo
self-drive

journey by car, which takes at least 3 hours. If you are still undeterred, be sure to book well ahead, as the services become full months in advance.

If you're intent on travelling by train, the **TGV** (the French intercity service) takes you more directly to Verbier. A service runs from Gare de Lyon in Paris via Lausanne (where you have to change trains) to Martigny from where you can get to Verbier by local train or bus or a taxi. The journey from Paris to Martigny takes around 5 hours with 4 services every day. To get to Paris, you can either fly or take the Eurostar.

by air

Another point in Verbier's favour is that the transfer from Geneva airport is noticeably shorter than to other popular resorts. There are daily scheduled flights to Geneva from all major UK airports (➡ planning your trip). Whichever form of transport you choose it should only take between 2-2½ hours. Once you have safely landed in Geneva, you can get to Verbier in one of 5 ways.

transfers

As the journey from Geneva by **car** takes just under 2 hours (approximately 105 miles) it is a feasible way to transfer to Verbier. You can hire a car at Geneva airport - book over the phone, on the internet, or when you arrive at the airport. Your car will have the necessary equipment required to legally travel on Swiss roads such as an emergency triangle and a vignette but you will need to specifically request snow chains and a roof box if you want them.

The **train** is an efficient and comfortable way to reach Verbier from Geneva airport, and the train station is conveniently placed next to the arrivals hall. Take any train going via Martigny - on average 2 direct trains run every hour from early morning until just before midnight and at least 1 non-direct service runs every hour with a change in either Geneva or Lausanne. At Martigny change onto the Grand St. Bernard Express to Le Châble, the last stop on the line. From the station in Le Châble, the Post bus (*Car Postale*) takes you to the main bus station in Verbier on Rue de la Poste. The whole journey takes about 2½ hours and costs CHF50-60 one-way. And in a welcome change from what you may be used to, the Swiss train timetable runs seamlessly - connections between trains can seem impossibly close so you may need to find the next platform quickly.

If you don't want to have to worry about driving yourself, there are a number of companies which run **private minibus transfers** from Geneva to Verbier. Services vary from a simple pick up and drop off to the provision of welcome packs and food and even champagne during your trip.

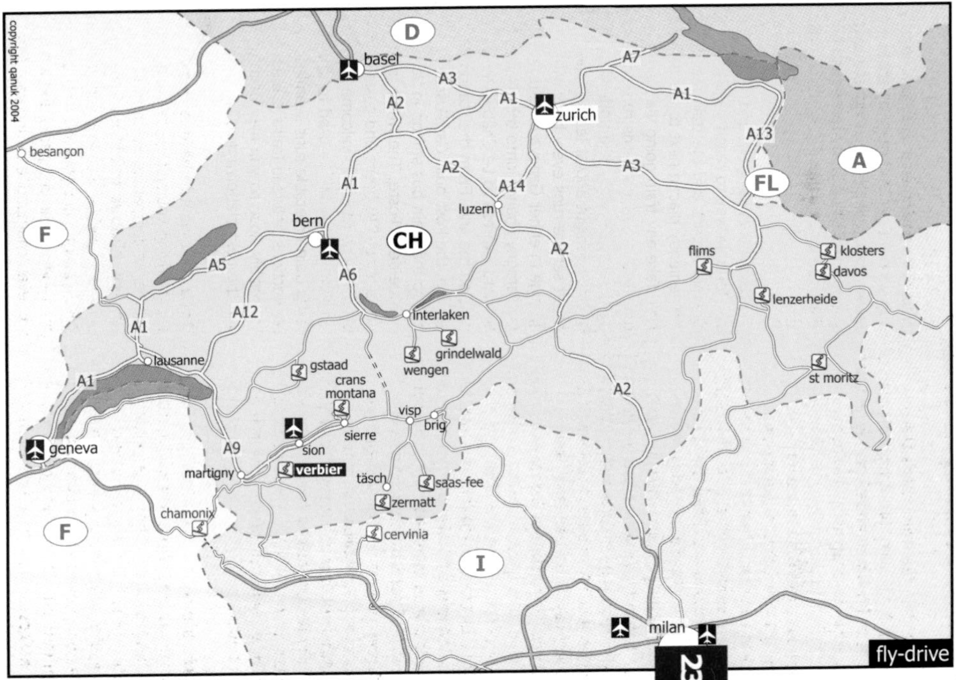

D
basel
A7
A3
A1
A2
zurich
A13
besançon
A2
A3
A1
A14
A
luzern
FL
F
bern
CH
A2
flims
klosters
A5
davos
A6
lenzerheide
A12
interlaken
A1
grindelwald
lausanne
gstaad
wengen
A1
crans
montana
A2
st moritz
visp
brig
sierre
geneva
A9
sion
martigny
verbier
täsch
saas-fee
zermatt
chamonix
F
cervinia
I
milan

There are a number of services, including ATS, Alp Line and Alpine Cab. All of them take online bookings, either via email or direct through the relevant website. You can only book the whole bus, which works out well cost-wise if you are travelling in a large group. Alpine Express, a transfer company based in Verbier, operates a **shuttle service** between the airport and the Place Centrale in Verbier. At the weekends, the service runs on average every 3 hours and during the week frequency depends on demand. A one-way ticket costs CHF75. Book before you arrive in Geneva. If you are travelling in a group too big for a minibus, hiring a private coach is an alternative - Lemania is a reputable company. **taxi** is an expensive alternative but if you are too tired to drive there yourself or have a phobia of public transport a one-way trip from Geneva airport will cost you approximately CHF650. If arriving in style is what counts, transferring by **helicopter** is also an option (bookable through Air Glaciers). The trip from Geneva to Verbier takes about 45 minutes. A helicopter can take up to 5 people and costs about CHF1500. The main drawback is that it is often adversely affected by bad weather and subject to cancellation.

Sion also has a small airport, which is a 40 minute drive from Verbier. Swiss operates a limited scheduled service from London Heathrow - with 1 flight every Saturday in each direction. From Sion you can get to Verbier by **train** - a service runs from Sion to Martigny twice an hour, and the journey takes about 15 minutes - or by **road**.

Once you've got to Verbier, getting your bearings is relatively easy - the only reason most skiers leave the village is to go home. Verbier is divided (by name at least) into a number of different districts, though some parts you are unlikely to visit unless you are staying there.

On the way up from Le Châble you pass through the confusingly named Verbier Village (the old village) before reaching modern day Verbier. The road up the mountain ends at the Place Centrale, the hub of Verbier and where a lot of the main action takes place. Home to the tourist office, 2 banks and a number of shops, restaurants, hotels and bars all the other main roads in and out of the village also begin or end here. Rue de Médran is where you will find the après scene and many of the hotels - the road climbs off to the right from the Place Centrale to the Médran lift station. Most skiers start their day at Médran and end it at the bottom of the blue run that finishes behind the lift station. The post office and main bus station lie on Rue de la Poste, which runs west from the Place Centrale. Keep going along this road and a turning on the right - Rue du Centre Sportif - leads to the Centre Sportif and the small district known as Patier.

The district known as Savoleyres - and where the other resort level lift station is found - is 1 km north of the Place Centrale, along Route des Creux.

snapshot

from verbier by road
4 vallées resorts
bruson 30 minutes
mayen de l'ours 1 hour 10 minutes
nendaz 1 hour 20 minutes
siviez 1 hour 30 minutes
thyon 1 hour 30 minutes
veysonnaz 1 hour 20 minutes

other resorts
chamonix (france) 1 hour
courmayeur (italy) 2 hours
crans montana 1 hour 20 minutes
saas fee 2 hours
super st. bernard 50 minutes
zermatt 2 hours 30 minutes

Beyond Savoleyres the road splits - right for Le Hameau (and the nursery slopes) and left for the higher parts of Savoleyres and Carrefour. In between Savoleyres and the centre of Verbier is an area that should be called 'chalet-land', as that is mainly what you will find there.

Because of the sprawling nature of the resort most visitors need some transport to get between the lift stations, restaurants, shops and après. If you don't have a car you can walk, catch a bus or a taxi. If you decide when you get to Verbier that you need a car, you can hire one (➥ the directory). If you venture round Verbier **on foot** the first thing you'll realise is that it has lots of hills. Shortly after that you'll realise that an efficient **bus** runs around the village. Regular, reliable and free this circulates Verbier 8am-7pm. You rarely have to wait for more than 10 minutes for a bus to turn up and in peak weeks they come more frequently though they are more busy. Buses loop around the resort to one of 4 destinations - no.1 runs to Carrefour via Savoleyres, no.2 to Le Hameau and Les Esserts, again via Savoleyres, no.3 to Patier, past the Centre Sportif, and no.4 to Verbier-Village. All buses stop at the Place Centrale and Médran.

If you like your personal space you can take a **taxi**. An expensive way to get around Verbier, but after the free buses stop at 7pm, it can be an essential means of transport for those staying far from the village centre. The directory lists some of the English-speaking taxi drivers operating in Verbier or alternatively you can ask at the tourist office for a full list.

If you are **driving**, navigating your way on these roads is relatively easy. All roads except Route des Creux are one-way, most landmarks are well signposted and traffic only builds up at weekends. Parking, on the other hand, is difficult at any time. There are large pay & display car parks at Médran and Savoleyres and the Centre Sportif (free), but very few parking spaces in the centre itself.

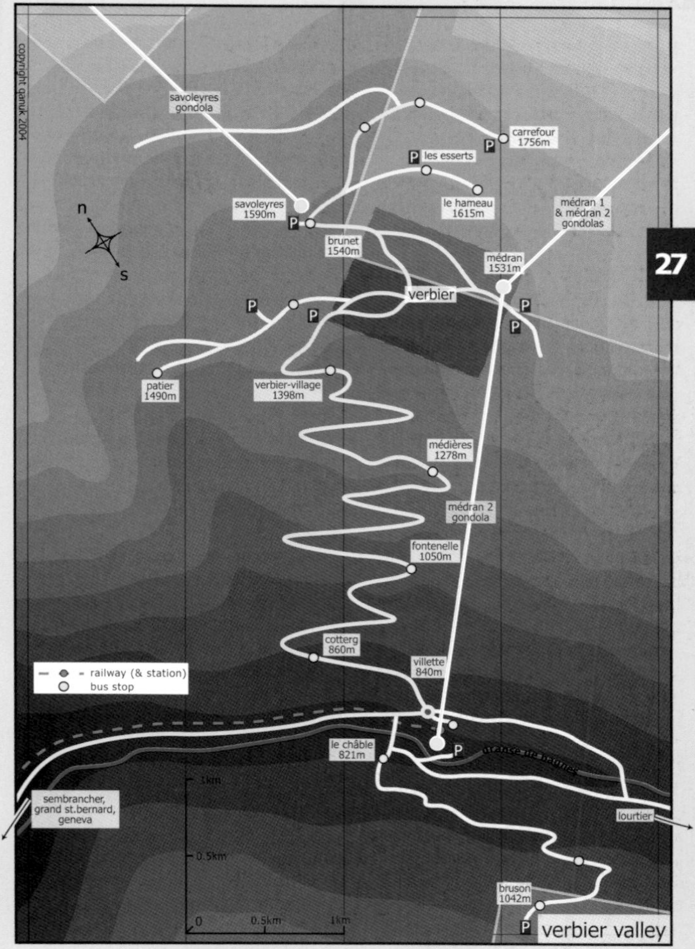

verbier valley

savoleyres gondola
carrefour 1756m
les esserts
le hameau 1615m
savoleyres 1590m
brunet 1540m
médran 1 & médran 2 gondolas
médran 1531m
verbier
patier 1490m
verbier-village 1398m
médières 1278m
médran 2 gondola
fontenelle 1050m
cotterg 860m
villette 840m
le châble 821m
sembrancher, grand st.bernard, geneva
lourtier
bruson 1042m

n
s

railway (& station)
bus stop

0
0.5km
1km

At the end of a day on the slopes, you probably won't mind where you rest your head. But when planning your holiday, you might want to put more thought into where you stay.
Verbier has a wide range of accommodation - 27 hotels from 2* to 5*, more catered chalets than any other resort, a few apartments and even a hostel.

Little of Verbier's accommodation is ski in/ski out. If you don't have a car, and don't want to trudge around the resort in ski boots, choose somewhere near Médran or Savoleyres and/or a bus stop. Accommodation is normally available from mid-December until late April, with availability best at the start and end of the season.

Though overall accommodation isn't cheap, there is something aimed at all budgets. Prices rise in the peak weeks and are at their lowest at the beginning and end of the season. Some accommodation - hotels, apartments, private guestrooms and chalets - can be booked through the tourist office, either by telephone or on their website.

hotels

One word - expensive. And it's debatable whether you get value for money. As in England, Swiss hotels are graded from 1* to 5* - but here the similarity stops. Stars are awarded for factors such as room size and whether the hotel has a restaurant offering an evening meal. The facilities one 4* hotel offers can be very different from another, depending upon how it earned its stars. On appearances alone it is often difficult to work out exactly what you'll get - price is generally the best guide. Each hotel has its own character and atmosphere - often the more you pay, the more formal it will be, from the restaurant to the service throughout. Some of the hotels are called garnis - and are more akin to a large scale b&b as that is the only type of board available. Hotels proper will offer b&b and half board (and sometimes full board) and a wider range of facilities. Some of the hotels also have '*résidences*' - apartments equipped for self-catering, though you can still make use of the hotel facilities.

specifics

Big or small? Old or new? Whether your taste is for service on tap or taps that need servicing, the hotels we review are those worthy of special mention. Unless otherwise stated, all bedrooms are en-suite, with a shower or bath and all hotels have a lift, and parking in either a private car park or the hotel garage.

You can make a **booking** with the hotel direct, or book through a tour operator or travel agent. The tourist office offers week packages (Saturday to Saturday) during low and mid season for some of the hotels - book by phone or through the tourist office website. Most of the hotels will only consider a booking for

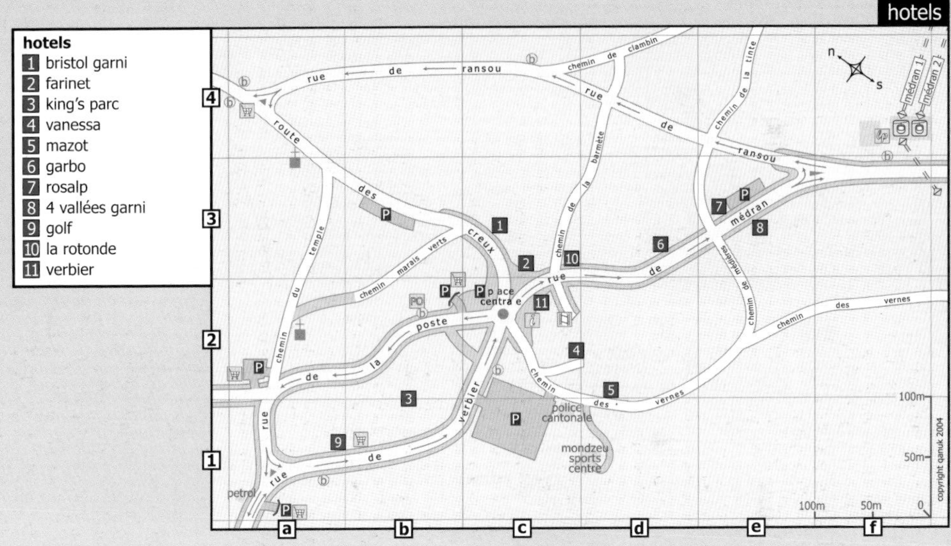
hotels
1 bristol garni
2 farinet
3 king's parc
4 vanessa
5 mazot
6 garbo
7 rosalp
8 4 vallées garni
9 golf
10 la rotonde
11 verbier
rue de ransou
chemin de clambin
route des creux
chemin du temple
chemin marais verts
chemin de la barmète
chemin de la tinte
rue de médran
chemin de médières
chemin des vernes
rue de la poste
rue de verbier
place centrale
police cantonale
mondzeu sports centre
petrol
médran 1
médran 2
n
s
100m
50m
0
copyright qanuk 2004
a
b
c
d
e
f
1
2
3
4

less than a week if it is made within 2 weeks of the date you want to arrive. As a general rule though, booking policies are most flexible during low season. None of Verbier's hotels are **ski in/ski out** so it tends to be a choice between being best placed for one of the resort lift stations or best placed for the bars and restaurants. Unlike resorts such as Courchevel, none of the hotels have an in-hotel **rental shop** - though many have a deal with a specific shop which they will advise you ofwhen you check in. Every front-of-house employee will speak **english**, but they are more than willing to humour your GCSE French if you want to give it a go.

prices

In this guide hotels are divided into 3 price categories - what you can expect to pay for a double room per night in high season, including tax but not service.

luxury - above CHF400
mid-range - CHF200-400
budget - below CHF200

Within these categories, most hotels also have low, mid and high season rates. Prices rise in peak weeks and are at their lowest at the beginning and end of the season. Some have a Christmas/New Year band as well, when prices are at their highest. All hotels accept most credit cards.

snapshot

for...

a last minute deal - bristol garni
central luxury - king's parc
families - vanessa
good food - montpelier
liveliness - farinet
location, location - rosalp
peace & quiet - les 4 vallées
star counting - chalet d'adrien
weekend availability - les rois mages

<< luxury >>

chalet d'adrien*****

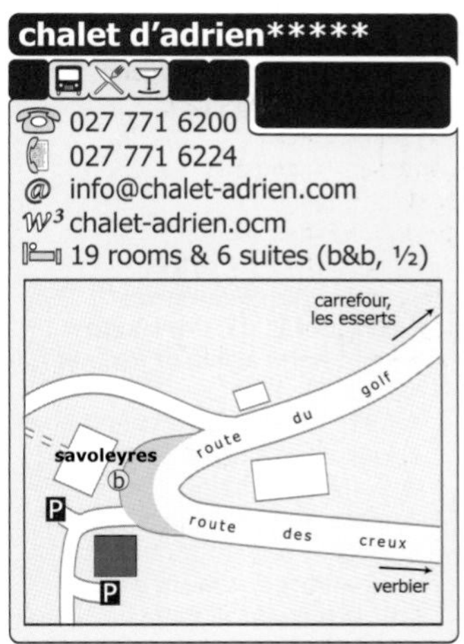

☎ 027 771 6200
027 771 6224
@ info@chalet-adrien.com
W3 chalet-adrien.ocm
19 rooms & 6 suites (b&b, ½)

Verbier's only 5* hotel, and with a price tag to match. A Relais & Chateaux, it is small and luxurious, and is perched above the village next to Savoleyres - which some may find inconvenient for the shops and restaurants. But you need not worry about going hungry - the hotel has 2 restaurants, L'Astrance for haute cuisine and Le Grenier for less extravagant dining, and on sunny days lunch is served on a expansive terrace with a hard-to-beat view up the valley. Rooms are individually and tastefully furnished and most face south. The hotel also has an appealing sauna, hot tub and hammam that will look after your aches and pains at the end of the day.

king's parc****

p29 b1/2

☎ 027 775 2010
027 775 2034
@ info@kingsverbier.ch
W3 kingsverbier.ch
26 (b&b, ½)

Behind the similarly-owned Hotel Rhodania, the King's Parc is in the heart of the village, but it is a 20 minute uphill walk to Médran if you don't take the hotel's free shuttle. All rooms are spacious suites and each has a living area in addition to the bedroom. On a cold and snowy day, it can be hard to get beyond the inviting lobby and lounge, with its log fire, well-stocked bar, comfortable leather chairs and a tempting cake trolley in the afternoon. The hotel houses an excellent, highly rated restaurant - also called King's - which offers a menu of "modern food with pacific-rim influences". Enough said.

rosalp****

p29 e3

☎ 027 771 6323
027 771 1059
@ rosalp@verbier.ch
W3 rosalp.ch
23 (b&b, ½)

Another Relais & Chateaux, the Rosalp is Verbier's best known 4* hotel. Opened in the 1940s by the Pierroz family, it is now famous for Roland Pierroz, its Michelin starred chef and owner. Centrally located in the heart of the shops, restaurants

verbier lodge***

Opened in 2003, the Lodge is a sport hotel aimed at serious skiers. Tucked away in the forest to the east of the village, it is only a 5 minute walk from Médran. You can reserve accommodation only or opt for one of the board & ski packages, which include ski instruction.

Rooms are named after different ski resorts - so let them know your favourite if you have one... although for an unimpaired view of the surrounding valley, a room on the second floor or higher is best. There are 3 suites, and some rooms have balconies. Apart from one of the suites, all other rooms only have a shower, so those who need a bath-tub to ease away their aches and pains will be disappointed. That said, the sauna, hammam and outdoor hot-tub help bring some relief and are more luxurious than the 3* rating suggests. There is also a small gym for those wanting to get in some last minute fitness training.

The Lodge makes a slightly optimistic bid to promote its bar for après-ski - you can ski to it by following the signs on the blue piste down to Médran - but residents may be keen for it to remain a secret, as it is a pleasant spot for a drink, and is far from the madding crowd in the centre of the village.

and bars, it is less than a 5 minute walk from Médran. Of all the 4* hotels, the Rosalp takes itself the most seriously and the atmosphere is more reserved and more formal than elsewhere. Some bedrooms would benefit from being a little bigger but the rest of the facilities are top-class - guests with weary muscles from a tough day on the slopes will enjoy the leisure facilities and the attentions of the in-house masseur.

montpelier****

027 771 6131
027 771 4689
@ hotel-montpelier@verbier.ch
W3 hotelmontpelier.ch
46 (b&b, ½

centre sportif
verbier
chemin de plan pra
P
sportif
centre
du
patier
rue
chemin de plan pra

The Montpelier's only drawback is its location - it's a 30 minute walk to either of the Médran or Savoleyres lift stations and 20 minutes to the centre - but the excellent facilities mean you only need to leave to go skiing. The hotel has a spa with a small indoor pool where you can swim whilst admiring the view, large bedrooms decorated in stencilled wood, and one of the finest restaurants in Verbier, which serves excellent haute cuisine food. The best room is the magnificent penthouse, which has its own log fire. But if that's beyond your budget, you can warm yourself by the one in the lounge. Service throughout is polite and unobtrusive.

<< mid-range >>

vanessa****

p29 c2

027 775 2800
027 775 2828
@ vanessa@verbier.ch
W3 -
55 (b&b, ½)

One of Verbier's larger hotels, the Vanessa is ideal for families, or groups of friends who want to stay in a hotel - some of its duplex apartments can sleep up to 6, though smaller rooms are also available. Despite needing a decorative overhaul to bring it into the 21st Century, the family-like atmosphere is what brings people back - service is quirky but friendly and you'll soon feel more like a good friend than a guest. Located just off the Place Centrale and only a 10 minute walk from the Médran lift station, most of Verbier's attractions are within easy reach. If you self-drive, you can park for a small daily fee in the hotel garage.

les 4 vallées garni****

027 775 3344
027 775 3345
@ les4vallees@verbier.ch
W³ les4vallees.com
20 (b&b)

A very good value choice, the 4 Vallées is a small, friendly, family-run hotel. Only breakfast is served, but as it is located on Rue de Médran, there are plenty of restaurants nearby. The en-suite rooms are reminiscent of the 1970s, with avocado bathrooms and orange and brown furnishings, but the cleanliness and warmth more than compensate. Most rooms face south and have stunning views over the valley. Nothing is too much trouble - your ski boots are dried overnight, and the cosy bar will stay open as long as you need it to. Sadly for animal lovers, pets are not allowed.

bristol garni***

027 771 6577
027 771 5150
@ hotel.bristol@verbier.ch
W³ bristol-verbier.ch
31 (b&b)

An ideal hotel for those wanting to be close to the action without paying over the odds. The Bristol is located just up from the Place Centrale on Route des Creux. Everything you need is on the doorstep - Borsalino or Le Caveau for eating (➥ eating out), the Farinet for drinking and Tara's (underneath the hotel) for dancing (➥ après-ski & nightlife). The hotel was renovated in 1999 and though the rooms are sparsely furnished they are clean and of an ample size. In the reception there is a free internet connection and a surprising amount of information about Sweden.

les rois mages****

027 771 6364
027 771 3319
@ info@skiverbier.com
W³ skiverbier.co.uk
15 (b&b)

The 'Wise Kings' is a curiosity in Verbier, being the only hotel run by a ski company (Ski Verbier). Having only 15 bedrooms, it feels more like a chalet than a hotel, which in some ways is reflected by the service you receive. In the hotel itself, the managers look after your needs whilst the other aspects of your holiday - such as lift passes and lessons and a shuttle service around the resort - are organised by the Ski Verbier reps. Located a 2 minute walk from the distinctive Catholic church, the Rois Mages welcomes weekend stayers and has a flexible booking policy should you wish to stay for less a week. Families are welcome - during school holidays special evening meals and babysitting services are available on request, and there is a playroom for children.

farinet***

At the heart of the village above the Place Centrale, the Farinet is better known for après-ski. The rooms are comfortable, although some have been more recently renovated than others. The hotel is reasonably well sound-proofed, but if you are a light sleeper or an afternoon napper, ask to be on a higher floor, so you're not disturbed by noise from the bar. The atmosphere is youthful - perhaps created by the staff, most of whom are in their 20s or 30s. The lounge bar on the ground floor was recently revamped and you may feel you've been transported to a drinking venue in London - and as such is a slightly odd setting for your breakfast - but comes into its own when the clock strikes après.

le mazot***

p29
d2
5
027 775 3550
027 775 3555
@ mazot@verbier.ch
W3 hotelmazot.ch
25 (b&b, ½)

Mazot means 'Swiss Home', and accordingly you will feel welcome as soon as you arrive. A long corridor of a hotel, there are fewer bedrooms than the building size suggests, so you have plenty of space. The staff are extremely friendly and helpful and speak good English. The hotel is a 2 minute walk from the Place Centrale, 10 minutes from Médran, and the Mondzeu swimming pool is just across the road. You can park for free outside the hotel, or in its garage for a small daily fee. Other facilities include a sauna, a solarium and a free internet connection in the hotel lobby.

<< budget >>

garbo**

None of Verbier's hotels are truly 'budget' - some are cheaper than others, but few are good value. Garbo's wins inclusion because of its location - 5 minutes from the Médran lift station and in the middle of the après-ski fun (including the hotel's own bar), meaning you will rarely be alone. As it is less frequently used by tour operators than other hotels, the atmosphere is more personal. The bedrooms are small and contain the bare essentials - and have little space for much else. A good continental breakfast is served in what becomes Garbo's restaurant in the evening.

the bunker

027 771 6602
027 771 6603
@ sleep@thebunker.ch
W3 thebunker.ch
3 dormitories (½)

Truly a budget offering, the Bunker is a hostel rather than a hotel. Located in the Centre Sportif, accommodation is available in one of 2 very different buildings. The Bunker itself is an old nuclear shelter, with 5 entirely underground dormitories - though you'll never see the sun at least you know you'll be safe in the event of an atomic attack. For the princely sum of CHF45 you get a bed (for which you need to bring your own sheets) free entrance to the swimming pool and ice rink, breakfast, a 3-course evening meal, and digital TV and video. Accommodation in dormitories or double rooms is also available in the nearby Summer House. Slightly more expensive than the Bunker, perhaps because of the need to clean and maintain windows, priority is given to 1 week rentals.

and the rest

The 3* hotel **golf** (t 027 771 6515, i golfhotelverbier.ch) on Rue de Verbier is one of the better hotels in this star bracket. The hotel **la rotonde** (t 027 771 6525, i hotelrotonde.ch) above the Millennium restaurant on Rue de Médran and the ever bustling hotel **verbier** (t 027 775 212, i hotelverbier.ch) on the Place Centrale are well situated for those wanting to be fully involved in resort life.

chalets

Chalet holidays cater for those who want to stay in a more relaxed setting, but don't want to fend for themselves. And Verbier has them in plenty from the luxurious Descent-managed Septieme Ciel to more basic offerings from mainstream operators. Most chalets are situated between Savoleyres and the resort centre - and development is moving increasingly away from the heart of the village.

tour operators

There are plenty of English tour operators offering chalet holidays to Verbier. The chalets on offer are a mix of detached houses built in the traditional chocolate box style and an apartment (a series of rooms) on 1 or 2 floors of a larger building. Either way, the most commonly available chalet package includes bed, breakfast, afternoon tea, and on 6 nights out of 7 an evening meal with wine. You will be looked after by at least 1 English chalet host. Mainstream operators also organise flights and transfers. The more you pay, the better you can expect the quality of everything to be. Some companies offer discounts to big groups and families. Unless you book the whole place you take pot-luck with your fellow guests - it can be a war-zone or the beginning of a beautiful friendship - but at least you know you all like snow.

independents

Information on privately run chalets is not as easy to find, although the internet is a good place to start - some owners have their own websites or list their chalets on sites such as ifyouski.com. Interhome (t 0208 891 1294, i interhome.co.uk) also maintains a huge database of privately-owned accommodation and lists over 30 properties in Verbier. The Verbier tourist office publishes a list for the upcoming season in mid-July of the private chalets available to rent. This gives you contact details for the chalet owner or managing agency so you can deal with them directly. Or you can contact one of the many accommodation agencies based in Verbier - including Domus (t 027 771 6969, i agencedomus.ch), Valena Location (t 027 771 6565, i agence-valena.ch) and V.F.P (t 027 775 3010, i vfp.ch).

What is on offer in privately run chalets varies greatly. Some provide a similar package to those run by tour companies, some are bed & breakfast only, and in some you are left entirely to your own devices - about the only place in Verbier where you can take a room on a nightly basis is the privately run verbier chalet.

apartments

If an estate agent had to describe a typical ski apartment, 'compact and bijoux' would most likely be the phrase. An apartment for 4 is generally 2 rooms (a bedroom and living room), with 2 guests sleeping on a sofa-bed. They are on the face of it the cheapest place to stay - but when you add in the price of food and meals out, you can pay more overall than you would pay for a hotel or chalet. However if you can live like a sardine and stay disciplined about what you spend on food, it can be cost-effective.

Verbier only has a handful of such accommodation. The list of chalets kept by the tourist office also includes apartments available for short or long term let, or again you can use one of the accommodation agencies. Some tour operators - including Ski Armadillo, Sports Travel Company or Mountain Beds - rent accommodation-only apartments.

Wherever you stay you can expect to be provided with kitchen facilities and utensils, along with bed linen and a simple kitchen kit. In the most basic apartments this means a fridge, a hob, pots and pans, a few knives and forks and some washing-up liquid. Luxuries like TV connection are extra. In the most upmarket options you will have things like a microwave and widescreen TV, and pleasant little touches like coffee and hot chocolate in the cupboard. And wherever you stay is likely to be immaculate, and you will be expected to return it in the same state - an extra charge will be levied if the agency doesn't think your cleaning skills are up to scratch!

Prices vary depending upon whether it is high, mid or low season. As a guide, a short-term let for a mid-grade apartment with 2 rooms (4 beds) costs approximately CHF2800 in peak weeks and CHF1200 in low season. Some apartments are available on a long-let if you want a place for the season - the demand is high for these so make sure you book early.

mountain huts

If you want to have a go at living like the early alpinists, Verbier is one of the few resorts where you can stay in a mountain hut without too much effort. Two huts are within lift access of the village. Of these the most popular is the **cabane du mont-fort** (t 027 778 1384), which is open year round and can accommodate 58 people overnight. Sleeping arrangements are cosy - dormitory style - but if the weather closes in you may be glad of it. During the evening you can tuck into a delicious fondue and copious amounts of red wine and then awake in the morning to crowd-free pistes. Reservations are essential. The alternative is the smaller **cabane du tortin** (t 027 288 1153) just below Mont Fort at the top of the Glacier draglift - dinner and accommodation are similar.

cheaper options

Staying in Le Châble at the bottom of the valley (altitude 850m) is an altogether cheaper option. Although you're not staying in the heart of the action, you may find that you actually get to the skiing more quickly than somebody staying in the environs of Verbier - it's only a 7 minute ride on the Médran gondola and it means you get to queue-jump the lines of skiers waiting at Verbier's main lift station. You can only ski down to the village from the ski area when conditions are exceptionally good - otherwise the easiest way home is down in the lift. The lift runs until early evening (7:30pm) so you can get back up to Verbier for dinner and the nightlife - as long as you have made alternative plans for getting home. After dark in Le Châble is undisputedly quieter, though as more and more ski instructors and long-term seasonnaires are being priced out of Verbier, things are livening up. Along with a handful of hotels and b&bs, one accommodation option is the English-run Chill Inn (t 0041 788 348033, i chillinnverbier.com) a private chalet, which sleeps up to 10 and has its own hot tub.

For the truly hardcore there is also a caravaneige site in Le Châble (t 027 776 2051), which has water and electricity points.

If you're prepared to spend a bit of time you can also find accommodation in one of the other resorts attached to the 4 Vallées ski area. Though there are package deals aplenty to Verbier from the UK Nendaz is the only other resort currently covered by (a handful of) UK tour operators - so for the rest you will have to arrange it yourself. Interhome is a good starting point for finding chalet or apartment accommodation. Each resort has good and bad points - Nendaz is ideal for children and families, Thyon being at 2000m is snowsure and ski in/ski out and the smaller villages of Veysonnaz and Mayen de L'Ours are smaller but more charming. Overall accommodation and eating out is better value for money (though the choice can be more limited) and you get access to the same ski area.

Once you've arrived in Verbier and found where you're staying, there are a few things to do before you can get onto the slopes. For many people, long queues and language barriers make this the worst part of the holiday. Starting with lift passes, the following pages take you step by step through the process and how to survive it.

What kind of lift pass you buy dictates whether you find Verbier's lift pass system very efficient or very tiresome. You need your pass at the bottom of every lift in the 4 Vallées - but if you buy one for 3 days or longer it contains a microchip that is scanned automatically by the blue screen at the lift gates. You don't even have to take it out of your pocket.

verbier or 4 vallées?

You have 4 options, depending upon where you want to ski. The 4 Vallées pass allows you to use all lifts within the skiable domain, from Thyon to Verbier, as well as 1 day's skiing in either Chamonix or the Val d'Aosta in Italy. Beginners may only want a Verbier pass, which is good for Lac des Vaux, Les Attelas and La Chaux above the resort as well as the Savoleyres and Bruson areas. You can buy a lift pass covering just Savoleyres and Bruson or for Bruson only - with the latter you get 1 day's free use of the lifts in the nearby areas of Champex, La Fouly, Vichères, Les Marécottes and Super St. Bernard. Any of the lift pass options allows you to use the bus service that runs around Verbier for free.

snapshot

useful information

4 different lift pass types are sold - 4 vallées, verbier, savoleyres or bruson.
for a 3 day pass or longer, you need 1 passport sized photo.
there are discounts for families, under 21's, over 65's, groups and non-skiers.
you can buy your lift pass from 3pm the day before.

Three little-known ski pass packages are also available. The first is the Valais Ski Card, which works on a credit basis - 1 point of credit costs CHF1 (though if you buy a chunk of credit you get a discount on the price - the more you buy the bigger the discount). The credit is good for 2 years and with it you can ski in 28 resorts, including the whole of the 4 Vallées, Saas Fee, Crans Montana and Grimentz. Each day that you ski, and use the lift system lift, credit to the value of the sector you enter is debited from your card.

The second package, 'Around Mont Blanc', gives you 4 days in the 4 Vallées and 2 days of your choice in either the Aosta valley in Italy (including Courmayeur and Breuil/Cervinia) and the Chamonix valley (but excluding Les Houches) in France.

The final package is called 'Mont Blanc snow safari'. Consisting of 6 coupons you can ski in a different resort (again the 4 Vallées, the Aosta valley and the Chamonix valley) every day for 6 consecutive days - at your choice.

For all these passes, you need a passport photo and to produce proof of age.

handy to know

TéléVerbier (t 027 775 2511) runs and maintains Verbier's lift system and is responsible for all lift pass sales. The TéléVerbier offices at the Médran and Savoleyres lift stations open daily 8:35am-5pm. If you have booked an accommodation and lift pass package through the tourist office (➥ hotels), your pass will be waiting for you in your hotel when you arrive. If you have already got a smartcard (or a compatible Swatch watch) you can charge your ski pass on the internet through the TéléVerbier website (i televerbier.ch).

You can buy any pass for any number of days. It is more cost effective to buy 1 pass for all the days you plan to ski, as the overall cost decreases the greater the number of days you buy it for. So if you plan to ski for 6 days it is cheaper to buy a pass for 6 days than a day pass for each day. A 4 Vallées pass is the most expensive. If you buy a Verbier pass and later decide you want to ski Mont Fort, (or anywhere else in the 4 Vallées) you can buy a supplement at the Médran and Savoleyres lift stations or on the mountain at the bottom of the Jumbo or Gentianes cable cars. Be aware that for passes of 3 days or longer, the electronic smartcard used by TéléVerbier costs CHF5 on top of the lift pass price.

If you decide to buy a **day pass**, they are cheaper after 11am (a 'midi' pass) and cheaper still if bought after 12:30pm (a 'mini' pass). If you plan to visit Verbier several times during the season, buying a **season pass** can be the most cost effective approach.

Young adults - **under 21s** and **under 16s** - and older adults - **over 65s** - qualify for discounts (of varying amounts) - and **children** below the age of 5 ski free (but you still need to get them a pass). You need proof of age when you buy discounted passes. For a **family** - of 3 or more including 1 parent - travelling together and skiing for the same number of days, a family pass is the cheapest deal and includes unmarried 'children' aged 20 and under. **non-skiers** who want to use the lifts also get a discounted rate, as do large **groups** - of 20 or more - if all passes are bought at the same time for the same number of days. Boarders who care only about how much 'air' they get can buy a **snowpark** pass, at a reduced rate per day.

You can pay for all passes with cash or credit card (Eurocard, Visa, AMEX, Mastercard and Diners).

For ski passes for 3 days or more you need a **photo** - TéléVerbier can scan the picture from your passport onto the lift pass smartcard. If you come back to Verbier that year or in following seasons, you can re-use the same smartcard. If you have a Swatch watch with the Snow Pass system, your ski-pass can be loaded onto it. Lift passes are not transferable and you can be fined for using somebody else's pass - the lift operators sometimes make random checks.

Saturdays and Sunday mornings are a bad time to buy your pass as the **queues** can be very long. You can buy a ski-pass for 3 days or more after 3pm on the day before the first day you plan to use it.

TéléVerbier offers personal **insurance** - Verbier Securité - against accident on the slopes. This can be bought at the same time as you buy your lift pass. The insurance also covers lift closure, with certain conditions. If you lose a pass originally issued for 3 days or longer, or if you break your smartcard (even with a small crack the machines can't scan it), you can get a new one for a small charge. An Air Glacier card offers alternative insurance. Available from the lift pass offices a card covers the cost of any assistance you need for off-piste incidents, including blood-wagon and helicopter recovery.

What can often be a long-winded and tedious affair has been much improved in Verbier in recent years. Some shops are still small and stuffy, but service overall is faster and more friendly and almost all employees speak enough English to make sure you leave with what you want. As with buying your lift pass, if you avoid Saturdays and Sunday mornings, typically the busiest times, you shouldn't have to wait for hours.

handy to know

Getting the right equipment will ensure you fully enjoy your holiday. Your feet will hurt if you don't get well-fitting boots so don't be embarrassed to persevere until you find a pair that fits. If they cause you problems on the slopes take them back - all the shops will help you find a more suitable pair. Unless you know you want a specific type or make of ski, take the advice of the ski fitter. They are the experts and will know which is the best ski for you based on your ability and age.

At most shops you can take out **insurance** (except on test skis) to cover accidental breakage, loss or theft, though skiing on roads is not insurable! Unfortunately skis do get stolen or taken by accident - with so many people skiing on similar skis it's easy to confuse your skis with those belonging to somebody else. When you stop for lunch or après it's a good idea to swap one of your skis with a friend so you both have a mis-matched pair. This helps to ensure that nobody will pick up your skis, either by mistake or otherwise.

There is the usual extensive choice of rental shops with little difference between them. One reason to go to a particular shop is if your hotel or tour operator has arranged a rental deal with them - you may get a cheaper rate or insurance thrown in for free, so it's worth checking. Most shops stock a varied range of the latest ski equipment from all the usual manufacturers - Salomon, Völkl, Atomic, Rossignol and Dynastar. And because there are so many places to hire equipment, prices are competitive. A standard ski and boot package for 6 days costs about CHF200, whilst a premium package for 6 days costs about CHF270. Equipment for children is often available at a reduced rate - price is normally worked out on the basis of height rather than age. You can pay for your rental at the time you get your equipment or when you bring it back. If you pay upfront and then use your equipment for a shorter or longer period, the shop will make the necessary price addition or reduction when you take it back. In either case, you may have to leave a deposit and some shops may charge for ski pole hire. There's little to choose between most of the shops, so those overleaf are mentioned for their location, opening hours or excellent service.

for skis

no. 1 sports just along from the Médran lift station stocks an extensive range of skis which are well maintained and serviced. Another plus is that No. 1 only closes for a 1 hour (1pm-2pm) lunch break during mid-week - many other shops take a generous 3 hour siesta.

ski service next door to Le Fer à Cheval is part of the swissrentasport chain and lives up to its name, providing excellent and fast assistance. Staff are very friendly and speak good English and the range of skis for hire is extensive. They also stock an extensive range of clothes and accessories - the Patagonia and Quiksilver stores on the other side of the Rue are under the same management.

la boit askis is close to Médran and offers free storage to its rental customers.

For skiers staying in Savoleyres, **evasion sports** on Route du Golf is the only rental shop at that end of the village, but has a wide enough range of equipment to satisfy most needs.

for boots

If you are looking for your own pair of boots, the Canadian-born **surefoot** on Rue de Médran takes boot-fitting to a new art form. Using specially-designed technology they work out which is the best boot for you - selecting from a wide, which includes Salamon, Lange, Head and Atomic. Once chosen they customise the boots to fit as you want them to. Service is informative and very friendly.

Another option for custom-fit boots is **mountain air** - also on Rue de Médran opposite Le Fer à Cheval. The Welsh owner, Nick Hammond, is considered by many to be the best boot fitter in Verbier.

for boards

Though most of the ski shops also have a small range of boards for a better selection and more knowledgable service go to one of the 2 specialist boarding shops - the people serving you are more likely to be boarders and you're more likely to be able to get hold of a pair of Flow bindings and a pair of Spy goggles.

hardcore in the arcade on Rue de la Poste has a huge range of boards for rental and sale, including Burton, Salomon and Rossignol, with traditional or step-in bindings, as well as a small selection of skis. They also have a good service centre for any equipment in need of some tlc.

no bounds on Rue de Médran rents Option, Burton, Salomon, Nitro, Buzrun, K2 or Rome boards with traditional or step-in bindings. It stocks a good range of boarding accessories and clothing.

for other equipment

Rental shops offer a lot more than just skis and boards. Most stock a wide range of ski clothing - although brands differ from shop to shop so you will need to shop around if you are looking for a specific make - and all the accessories you can think of. There is little difference from what you would pay for the same clothes in the UK. You can also hire touring skis, telemarks, snowblades, avalanche transceivers, snowshoes... in fact more or less anything you might conceivably need or want for the great snowy outdoors. **mountain air** positions itself at the extreme end of the market and stocks the resort's best range of equipment for more adventurous skiing plans - including a wide range of off-piste skis and several ranges of technical clothing. You can also get hold of the same as well as touring skis and avalanche packs from **ski service** and **no. 1**. It is best to reserve any specialist equipment you need well ahead - particularly towards the end of the season as the stores get cleaned out within minutes of a snowflake falling.

ski schools

Unlike the ESF in France, no single ski school holds sway in Switzerland. This has allowed the market to develop healthily - modern approaches to ski teaching compete with more traditional methods and there is fierce but healthy competition for clients.

handy to know

group lessons are the cheapest way to learn to ski. All the schools run similar systems - when you book you will be asked your level of skiing so you can be put with a group of skiers of a similar standard to yours. Skiers are split into five ability levels, which is defined by the colour of piste you are comfortable skiing on or on your own assessment of your overall standard of skiing. As a guide, level 1 is for complete beginners, level 3 for skiers who can do parallel turns on blue piste and level 5 for good skiers in all conditions. In practice the divisions are not as accurate as they could be - some people overestimate their ability or misunderstand words like 'confident' and 'controlled', so to an extent the level of your group is pot luck. As long as you can distinguish whether you are a beginner, an intermediate, or an advanced skier you are likely to find yourself in roughly the right place. Group lessons generally run in the mornings and afternoons Monday to Friday, with groups as small as 3 or as large as 10 depending upon demand. If you have the money, **private lessons** are without question the way forward. Once you're past the basics, individual attention is the best way to significantly improve your technique and is often better value. If you can get a group of 4 or more the individual price is similar to the price for group lessons, with the advantage that you go where you want to go and practise what you want to practise. You can arrange where and what time you meet your instructor. If you meet at your accommodation your instructor will take you to the slopes, which at least means you'll find each other. Be aware if you ask for your 3 hour lesson to start at 10am, it will still finish at 12pm so your instructor can make his afternoon lesson.

Private and group lessons generally last for 3 hours, 9am-12pm or 1pm-4pm. You can book a private lesson for a whole day. In low season some of the schools will book a private lesson for 2 hours.

You can book lessons at the schools for **children** aged 3 years or over (➡ children). Children aged 12 or over are normally allowed to join the group lessons.

There are no **boarding** specific schools, but all of the ski schools offer lessons for those on 1 plank instead of 2.

prices are fairly competitive between the schools - group lessons cost around

CHF50 for a half-day and CHF200 for 5 half-days. A half-day private lesson for one or two people costs around CHF200 and CHF250 for three or four people and a full day costs around CHF350 for 1 or 2 people and CHF400 for 3 or 4 people. You can pay for your lessons in cash or by credit card. The price does not include personal insurance or a lift pass.

Either **book** before you get to Verbier - by email, fax or phone - or once you're in resort, in person at the ski school office. In peak season always pre-book, as there are not enough instructors to meet demand. To confirm your booking, the schools will need your name, level of ability and a credit card number.

All the ski schools have **meeting points** at Médran and Ruinettes and, for beginners, at Les Esserts. Make sure you check the starting point of each lesson with the ski school or instructor. Where the lesson takes place is rarely decided until the actual day, and depends on snow conditions and on the make-up of the group, so the end point will only be decided during the lesson. At the end of the lesson you're on your own.

In Switzerland, ski **instructors** can work without any qualifications, though all schools run pre-season training. Some schools are more stringent about hiring qualified instructors than others - to ensure you are taught by a qualified instructor ask when you book your lesson. Also due to this more relaxed policy you will find more English, Antipodean and Swedish ski instructors teaching in Verbier than in Austrian or French resorts. If you hire an instructor for a whole day, it is customary for you to buy them lunch - whether or not you tip is up to you.

Lessons take place **whatever the weather**, unless the entire lift system is closed in which case the schools will refund the full lesson price. They will also refund you if you are ill or have an accident and can produce a valid medical certificate. If you cancel a lesson for any other reason, most schools will charge you 50% of the full price if you cancel at least 24 hours before the lesson. Cancel within 24 hours and the schools expect full payment.

As well as ski lessons, each school runs a programme of **other activities** (➥ events & activities).

altitude

A new school established in 2002 by a group of Swiss and English instructors, including a former member of the UK mogul team. All of the instructors are English-speaking, coming mainly from England or Scandinavia and all of them are qualified. They train twice a week to develop their own skiing and to keep up-to-date with the latest ski techniques and teaching methods. In addition to the usual group and private lessons, Altitude runs all-female lessons with female instructors. Or if you want to try a little bit of everything, the school offers a 'snowsport cocktail' - 3 half-days of lessons in skiing, snowboarding and snowblading.

la fantastique

The supermodel of the ski schools, with instructors kitted out in distinctive red Prada ski suits and matching accessories. Private lessons are its speciality - group lessons are only available for children - and it has about 60 instructors, many of whom are English or English-speaking. It is also competent and experienced at co-ordinating lessons for corporate trips. If you are looking for lessons away from the markers, La Fantastique also has a large number of guides on its books - they offer a number of off-piste trips, including haute-route tours and outings to the St. Bernard refuge.

la maison du sport

G
027 771 3363
027 771 3369
info@maisondusport.ch
maisondusport.ch
médran, les esserts, les ruinettes

The 'House of Sport' (aka the Swiss Ski and Snowboard school) is the largest of the ski schools in Verbier - its instructors seem to take over the resort in peak weeks and of all the ski schools it bears the closest resemblance to France's ESF. With size comes the ability to run most types of lessons - including the usual format for groups and with particular emphasis on activities for children. Morning group lessons start at 9am, the same time as the other schools, but afternoon lessons start at 2pm. Maison du Sport is the only school to offer group lessons on Saturdays, an adult beginners lesson on Sunday mornings and lessons for handicapped skiers. The school has a large meeting point in the car park just beyond the Médran lift station. Service in the main office can be frustratingly slow, so only go when you have time to spare.

european snowsport

The new school kid on the block and another contestant from England. Run by a group of BASI qualified instructors (including a BASI trainer), ES are the men (and women) in black. In addition to the usual group and private lessons, the school runs a weekly programme of 1-day clinics - 'back on the snow' gets your legs warmed up or you can join the 'carving', 'bumps', or 'introduction to off-piste' sessions to learn about a new discipline. Women-only clinics are also an option. For children, there is the very popular 'Kids Academy' - for which it is essential to book ahead.

warren smith ski academy

079 359 6566
(UK) 01525 374757
admin@snowsportsynergy.com
warrensmith-skiacademy.com
-

If you don't want to waste precious hours on lessons or spend your holiday fighting for pride of place behind your instructor the Academy offers an alternative. Warren Smith is something of a celebrity in Verbier. One of the UK's leading professional freeskiers, he is a multi-qualified instructor who established the Academy after discovering the joys of freeride. The focus is on high-performance skiing - to help intermediate, advanced and expert skiers finesse and fine-tune their technique on moguls or steeps, in powder or when carving. The Academy runs several 5 day courses throughout the season - each day runs 10am-3pm. During the course every skier is videoed and assessed back in the classroom, where the biomechanics of skiing and other skills are also discussed. Alternatively, you can book a full day or half-day private lesson. Skiers keen to qualify as instructors can use the courses as preparation, the Academy also runs race training and there is a 9 week course for GAP year students. And once you are back in the UK you can hone your skills using the DVD and books produced by the Academy. The Verbier-specific tour operator Peak Ski offers package holidays to Verbier which include instruction with the Academy.

guides

The view from the resort is a mixture of groomed pistes and untouched terrain. By far the best - and safest - way to make the most of the latter is to hire a qualified mountain guide. As they have spent years getting to know and understand the mountain terrain, not only will they find the best powder but you can trust them to look after your security.

The difference between **guides** and **instructors** is fundamental - instructing is about 'how' and guiding is about 'where'. Ski instructors are not permitted to take you off-piste and you should not ask them to. In contrast the limiting factor with a guide is your own ability. If you are competent enough they will take you anywhere you want to go. There is no question of a guide's **ability**. Becoming one takes years and requires an intimate knowledge of everything the mountains have to offer particularly how to be safe in this notoriously unpredictable environment. Guides are not just expert skiers, first and foremost they are mountaineers: physically fit individuals, with extensive experience of mountain rescue, practice and procedure. They are also proficient rock and ice climbers and are competent and comfortable in all types of conditions. During the course of qualifying, they are tested on a wide assortment of skills including alpine technique, avalanche rescue and first aid, to name but a few. The very definition of a safe pair of hands. In Switzerland all qualified guides are registered with the Swiss Bureau des Guides (t 027 775 3364), which effectively acts as a job agency. Most guides can also be booked through one of the ski schools. In addition there are some independent guides such as **alpine guides** (t 079 446 2289, i swissguides.com), **mountain experience** (t 01663 750 160, i mountain experience.co.uk) and **olivier roduit** (t 079 206 9790/027 771 5317, i mountain-guide.ch).

And **what's on offer**? Most thing you can think of - including off-piste skiing, touring (for 1 day or more), rock-climbing, ice climbing, heli-skiing, snowshoe tours. Guides will also show you around the pistes - but don't expect them to be too excited about doing it. The hiring of a guide is not cheap, but it's worth paying the **price** to come back alive. Typically the bigger your group, the less you pay individually. A day's guiding for up to 5 people costs around CHF500. Guides can only be booked for a whole day.

Unlike in France, guides are not obliged to provide you with an avalanche transceiver, but they will not take you off-piste without one. You can hire transceivers from most of the ski shops, or the ski schools may loan you one if you can charm the receptionist sufficiently.

If you decide to hire a guide, don't underestimate how fit you need to be to get the most out of the experience. Whilst the guide will cater the day to the standard of the least able skier in the group, he may still lead you along some tiring traverses or climbs to reach the best snow.

Finally a word of warning - perhaps because of the type of skier Verbier attracts, seasonnaires do tout their services as on- or off-piste guides. Although they may charge less than a qualified guide, you employ them at your own risk. It takes years of experience and training in mountain safety to qualify as a mountain guide and whilst unqualified guides may be excellent skiers familiar with the off-piste runs, they may not know enough about the snow conditions and the mountain environment to be able to judge whether a particular route is safe to ski or what to do if something goes wrong. Unqualified guiding is illegal and deciding to hire one may cause your insurance cover to be invalidated. There is an element of danger in all skiing, but additionally so when off-piste. For a bit more money and peace of mind, hire a qualified guide who will know how to conduct a crevasse rescue.

snapshot

lessons are for wimps

Almost every skier would benefit in some way from the odd lesson but if you would like somebody to show you around the ski area without commenting on the weaker points of your parallel turn, there are a few options. Some UK tour operators offer a ski orientation day in their package. How often they show guests around the mountain is closely monitored by the resort. The rules do change, but generally the resort allows them to guide guests on-piste once a week - the guides will not take you off-piste. It's a good way to get some inside knowledge on the best runs, the quickest lifts and the most popular watering-holes.

The Ski Club of Great Britain bases a rep (t 079 580 3639) in many European ski resorts throughout the season and there is one in Verbier. They run a weekly on- and off-piste ski programme for Ski Club members - with some days aimed towards intermediate skiers and some aimed towards experts. Details of the different days are displayed in the tourist office and the Hotel de Verbier, where you can also meet the guide each day in the early evening.

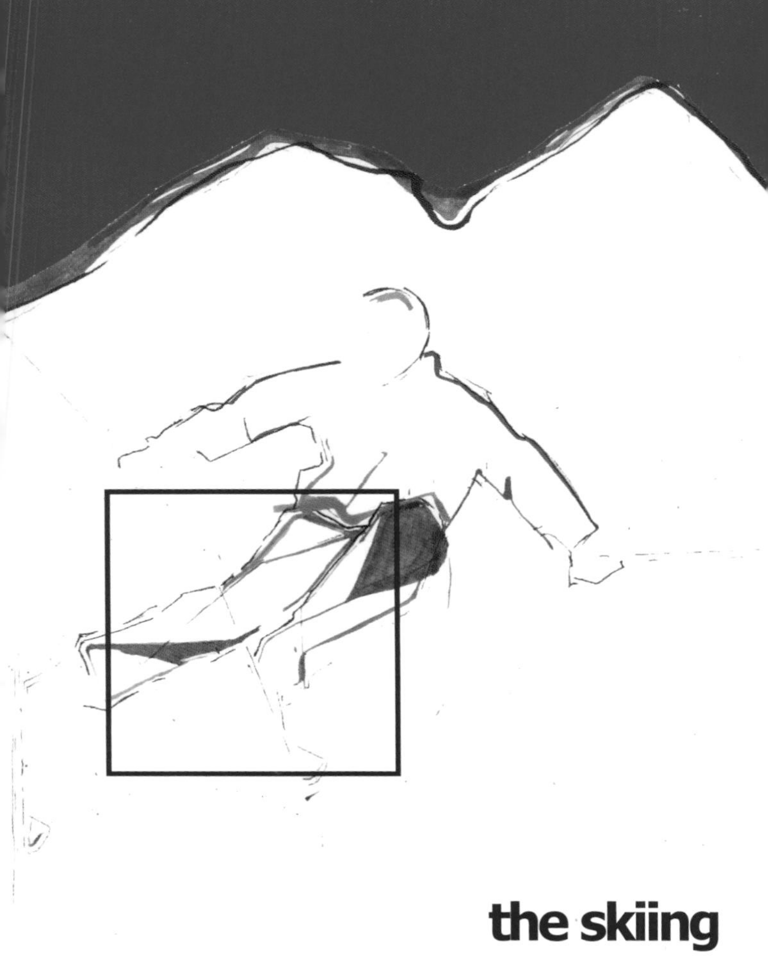

the skiing

The 4 Vallées is one of Switzerland's largest ski areas and offers everything from cruisey blues to nerve-testing high mountain tours. The size of the area, the variation of the pistes and the consistently good snow record has given the 4 Vallées a loyal following. The pistes probably offer most for intermediates whilst the off-piste area is a living dream for more advanced skiers and boarders. The longest vertical drop is 2500m, but take this with a pinch of salt - it is measured from the top of Mont Fort (3300m) to Le Châble (800m). Only expert skiers will enjoy the 18km descent - it includes the black mogul field at the top of Mont Fort and a technically demanding itinerary route from Verbier to Le Châble, which is only skiable where there has been an exceptional snowfall.

snapshot

vital statistics
410kms of pistes - 30 blues, 45 reds & 10 blacks
95 lifts - 11 buttons, 4 cable cars, 26 chairs, 24 drags & 10 gondolas
off-piste - 5 itinerary routes, 5 high mountain tours & vast unpisted backcountry
highest point - 3300m
longest run - 18kms

pistes

Though the pistes in the 4 Vallées are plentiful, a frequent complaint made is that the the runs are badly signposted and the piste map provided by the resort is difficult to follow. The pistes are numbered on the official piste map but not on the mountain, so it is not easy to work out which one you are skiing on.

You at least know when you are on a piste - the edges are marked by poles: on the left by a pole the colour of the piste with a small orange strip at the top and on the right by a half orange, half piste colour pole. The lifts are named, which helps a little, and a few yellow boards show the general direction of the resorts. Otherwise little guidance is given. The piste system adopts the same colour-coding used in all European resorts (➥ 'pistes' in the glossary) - but should only be used as a general guide. Although the gradient or width of each individual piste stays the same, other features such as snow conditions can change daily. A blue piste can become more testing than a nearby red, because it is over-crowded with skiers of ranging abilities or because of poor or icy conditions. And personal feelings about pistes vary greatly - an easy blue to one skier can seem like a vertical drop to another.

off-piste

In this guide we distinguish between the recognised and mapped itinerary routes and the rest of the off-piste found away from the lifts. Itinerary routes are identified by the colour yellow (on maps and the mountain) and though they are not groomed or checked at the end of the day, the resort classifies them as being "marked and protected from danger of high-altitude terrain". They will be closed if conditions are unsuitable - and for your own safety you should respect the signs. Alongside and in between pistes in most areas you will find plenty of ungroomed snow on which to practise your technique without going too far.

lifts

The lifts in the 4 Vallées are a hotchpotch of old and new. The companies of TéléVerbier, TéléNendaz, TéléThyon and TéléVeysonnaz are responsible for running and maintaining the lifts in their sector and they have different ideas about when and how much investment is required. In the last few years, TéléVerbier has made the biggest investment, so around Verbier there are more newer and faster lifts than elsewhere.

Most of the lifts open in early December - the remainder being operational by Christmas - and run until the middle or end of April. The exact date changes yearly and if the snow conditions are good, the lifts may open or close earlier than advertised. The lifts open later and close earlier during the shorter daylight hours in December, January and February. In March and April they generally open half an hour earlier and close half an hour later. Opening and closing times are noted at the bottom of each lift or you can get a full list of lift times from TéléVerbier. Wherever you ski, it is a good idea to work out which will be the last lift you will take to return home and check what time it closes.

the areas

For the purpose of the maps in this guide, the 4 Vallées has been divided into 8 sectors:
ruinettes (map a)
lac des vaux, attelas & la chaux (map b)
mont fort (map c)
siviez (map d)
thyon (map e)
nendaz (map f)
savoleyres (map g)
bruson (map h)
In this chapter you'll find a description of how to get to and from the slopes, the general characteristics and aspect of the area, and detail of the pistes, the off-piste and the mountain restaurants for each of these sectors. Maps a and b cover the ski areas immediately above the village, known individually as Attelas, Lac des Vaux and La Chaux (and known collectively as 'Verbier' for lift pass purposes). The upper section of 'Verbier' is shown on map b while the pistes below the Ruinettes mid-station are shown on map a. The description of 'attelas' in the following pages covers the lifts and pistes both above and below Ruinettes. At the back of this book there is a more detailed table of

lift information and the ski maps for each area (in which the piste colours correspond to those used by the resort) as well as a contoured overview of the ski area.

coming & going

The Médran lift station at the eastern end of the village is the starting point in Verbier for all the skiing in the 4 Vallées except for the Savoleyres and Bruson areas. All the village buses stop in front of Médran. If you come by car there are 2 car parks just beyond the lift station on either side of the road, which are pay & display 8am-4pm. At weekends the road to Médran becomes clogged with traffic, as visitors from Lausanne, Geneva and elsewhere pour into Verbier, meaning there is rarely a space in the car parks after 10am - so get there early. From Médran, you can get up the mountain in either of the inspirationally named gondolas, Médran 1 or Médran 2 - the latter starts in Le Châble. Both finish at 2200m at the mid-station known as Ruinettes. The entrance for the gondolas is the same - at the far end of the lift station if you approach it from the village - and opens at 8:45am. From that time until 11am at weekends and in peak weeks you can wait for up to 40 minutes to get into a lift. One way to bypass the queues is to do the round-trip down and back from Le Châble in the Médran 2 gondola - this is often quicker than standing in the queue - and always more pleasant, as you are guaranteed a seat. Immediately above Médran lies the area known as Attelas - from the top of which you can reach Lac des Vaux and La Chaux. Most skiers who start the day at Médran end it there - making the pistes down to the station busy in the afternoon. Those skiers staying near Les Esserts or Le Hameau can follow the pistes alongside the Bleu and Rouge draglifts to get home.

other resort-level lift stations

The other resort-level lift station in Verbier is at Savoleyres. This can also be reached by bus - nos.1 & 2 - and there is a car park at the side of the station. The quickest and most hassle-free way to get to the base station at Bruson is by car. Otherwise you have to rely on public transport, which is an efficient service if you time it well. Buses between Le Châble and Bruson run infrequently, with only ten services a day (the first from Le Châble at 8:45am and the last returning from Bruson at 5pm). The quickest way to get to Le Châble is down on the Médran 2 gondola. When the weather is bad and most of Verbier is trying to get to Bruson the buses are just too small for the quantity of skiers wanting to use them. On these days, either find a friend with a car, or stay in bed.

beginners

The nursery slope at Les Esserts keeps first-timers - and others - amused. It is the only suitable place for complete beginners and even then some may find the button lift daunting. And because of its low altitude the piste may be entirely made of artificial snow. There is a restaurant, which serves fairly standard fare, but the 'L'-shaped terrace is an ideal spot for parents or friends to watch from.

For newcomers to skiing, the Verbier experience may seem an ordeal. Unlike more purpose-built resorts, only those staying at the higher end of the village can walk to Les Esserts. The majority will have to use the bus service. Although this is reliable, when you are carrying skis, walking for the first time in extremely uncomfortable boots and trying to remember your goggles, gloves and hat, it can seem too much like hard work.

Beginners who have mastered the basics may find Verbier does not cater for them well either. The step from Verbier's nursery slope to Verbier's pistes is a big one - like skipping 'A' levels and going straight from GCSE to University - and whilst there are easy blue pistes in Lac des Vaux, La Chaux and Savoleyres, what you have to ski to get to them can be beyond the ability of less able or confident beginners. And once there, getting back down to the village can be just as tricky. If you want to avoid sliding down the hill on your backside, your only alternative way down is in the lift.

intermediates

By contrast the ski area is heaven for intermediate skiers. The pisted area is huge, with blue and red pistes in abundance. In a week's holiday you would be pushed to ski every one though marathon lovers will relish the challenge. Once you have found your ski legs, there are a decent number of black pistes on which to test your mettle.

experts

If you are an expert skier happy to hone your on-piste technique there is plenty to keep you busy. If you want to be pushed and tested at every turn, once you have skied the itinerary routes of Gentianes, Tortin and the mogul field at the top of Mont Fort, the pisted area may seem to offer little challenge. If this is the case, you would do well to hire a guide to show you Verbier's off-piste and backcountry area, which is almost as big as the pisted area.

boarders

Because it is easier to learn to board on a steep slope, novice boarders may cope better with Verbier's pistes than novice skiers and more experienced boarders will find plenty to entertain them. Skiers far outnumber boarders but because of the size of the area the two can get along quite happily. If you are a boarder who avoids drag or button lifts the Verbier sector is by far the most friendly. If you plan to explore the furthest extent of the ski area be aware that many of the essential links, especially to Thyon, are button or drag lifts, with no alternative. Getting across the area can also be tiresome as there are several long, flat paths. The same is true of the links to and from Nendaz - you must use 2 drag lifts.

the snowpark

The main attraction for boarders - and some skiers - is the sponsored snowpark at La Chaux (mysnowpark.ch). Sponsorship means investment which means that the park is well designed and well maintained. Allegedly there is also a snowpark under the Tournelle chairlift in the Savoleyres area but this is not always maintained or usable - check with TéléVerbier for info on their status or existence.

non-skiers

A popular pastime, particularly amongst the locals, even in the winter - as a non-skier, the first good reason to go up the mountain is to admire the spectacular view in every direction, while the second is to walk along the groomed and marked footpaths (of which there are over 25kms in total). With a lift pass (➥ lift passes) you can go up in any of the gondolas or cable cars, but not the chairlifts, drags or button lifts for obvious reasons. Wherever you walk, watch for out-of-control skiers - or tobogganers - flying past.

The starting point is Médran, the same as for skiers - take either gondola to Ruinettes. Once there you have 3 choices. You can go higher in the Attelas gondola and follow the path from there to the top of the Chassoure-Tortin gondola in which you can descend to Tortin. Another option is to walk down from Ruinettes along the blue piste which runs through the forest to Médran. The third walking route is from Ruinettes to La Chaux or you can take the strange caterpillar-tracked bus that runs between the 2 points - it is for pedestrians only and runs 9am-4pm. Once in La Chaux, it would be a shame not to carry on to the top of Mont Fort - take the Jumbo and then the Mont Fort cable car - to the large viewing platform from where you can admire the stunning vista of peaks. Once a week TéléVerbier organises a trip to the top for sunrise. On the Savoleyres side, once up the mountain in the Savoleyres gondola you can descend to La Tzoumaz in its gondola or walk down to the Sky Bar. From Carrefour, you can walk up the route of the same name - if it is open - to Marmotte. If your legs need a break by the time you get back down the Restaurant Carrefour can give you a restorative drink and the no.1 bus can take you back to the centre of Verbier.

The main (and the middle) valley in the Verbier sector - its pistes start as high as 2723m and run all the way down past the Ruinettes mid-station to Verbier. It is by far the busiest valley of the three - in the morning all skiers use its lifts to reach Lac des Vaux, La Chaux, Nendaz, Siviez and Thyon and then ski its pistes at the end of the day to return from these areas to the town. When Route Carrefour is open skiers returning from Savoleyres also ski the lower pistes below Ruinettes. The upper pistes are graded red or black, so only reasonably competent (or confident) intermediate skiers will cope with them and at the end of the day they can be littered with struggling skiers.

Most of the slopes in Attelas face south-west. Combined with the volume of traffic, conditions in this area are generally poorer than elsewhere, particularly below Ruinettes. There are several snow-making machines, which work hard to keep snow levels topped up - but even with these the pistes can be poorly covered at the end of day or the beginning or end of the season.

access

From Médran, take either gondola to Ruinettes. To reach the top from there take the Funispace or Attelas 2 gondola, the latter being slower but often quieter. Both end on the ridge between Lac des Vaux and Attelas, though at slightly different points.

map a & b

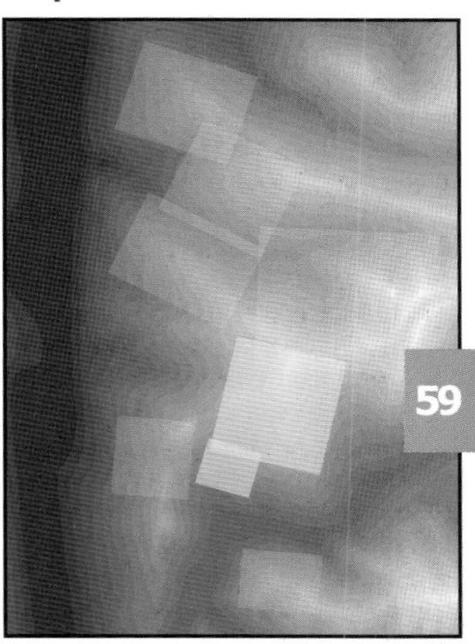

snapshot

out of interest
highest point - 3023m
aspect - sw
lifts - 4 buttons, 7 chairs & 4 gondolas
pistes - a lone blue, variable reds & testing blacks
off-piste - 1 itinerary route & 2 high mountain tours
restaurants - 6

highlights & hotspots
numerous spots for après
queues at the beginning of the day
busy slopes at the end of the day
mont gelé

pistes

The only **blue** in the area is the gentle path that runs through the forest from Ruinettes down to Médran (➥ getting home).

In contrast Attelas has **red** pistes galore. The main descent from the top of Attelas is red - you can reach it from the top of the Funispace or the top of the Attelas 2 gondola - and offers a range of routes down. Coming from the top of the Funispace, the left piste is a narrow flatish path whilst the right side is a steeper wider slope. Lower down it splits - the left route is steep and often icy whilst the right is a narrow path. From there you can ski to the bottom of the Combe 2 chairlift, or turn off to La Chaux or to Ruinettes. The generally heavy traffic and consistently poor snow conditions on the lower section doesn't make this a piste you ski for enjoyment's sake. If you do want to ski the upper part again it is better to go back up in the Combe 2 or Attelas 3 chairlifts as both are normally quieter than the lifts from Ruinettes. The piste from the top of Combe 2 is also red, a flat and narrow path to start with before widening into a fairly steep slope. The lower reds to the bottom of the Mayentzet and Combe 1 chairlifts are ideal for intermediates wanting to do laps to practise their technique.

There are 2 **blacks** in this area. The first and longest is narrow and steep - it

starts at the top of the Funispace, sweeping down Attelas from underneath this lift to the bottom of the Mayentzet chairlift. The first 20 metres or so can be bare or heavily mogulled, but beyond that the run is smooth and fast. The piste is often used for competitions during which time it is closed to the public. The second black is shorter and starts just below Ruinettes, although the top section is not always groomed. It also ends at the bottom of the Mayentzet chairlift.

off-piste

The only **itinerary route** starts at the top of the Fontenay chair. A relatively short descent it is often mogulled but is a good place to test your technique without exhausting yourself before trying the longer, more testing itinerary routes elsewhere.

For expert skiers, the **high mountain tours** of the majestic Mont Gelé peak that dominates Attelas is the main draw. To reach the top, take the Mont Gelé cable car, which starts next to the top of the Funispace. The lift closes in high winds or when the conditions on this notoriously testing mountain are too difficult or unsafe. From the top you can ski the most popular route - down towards Tortin - or the south face to La Chaux. The extreme couloirs visible from Attelas are rarely skied, except during the Verbier Ride (➥ events & activities), when professional freeriders hurtle down at unbelievable speeds.

As you ascend in the Funispace, you will notice several extreme and avalanche prone couloirs. Known as Creblet and Rock and Roll this is off-piste proper and the descents are for true experts only - though you'll see the tracks, you'll rarely see the skier.

eating & drinking

attelas (t 027 771 3291) is a small self-service restaurant at the top of the Attelas 2 gondola. The outside terrace is perfect for soaking up the sun under the gaze of Mont Gelé. During the Verbier Ride (➥ events & activities), it is used by the event organisers and members of the press.

The restaurant **carrefour** (t 027 771 7010) (➥ eating out) lies at the end of bus route no.1, but you can reach it on skis from Attelas and from Savoleyres if Route Carrefour is open. Its proximity to a bus-stop also makes it a good place for some wobbly après and to meet non-skiing members of your party.

chez dany (t 027 771 2524) is a Verbier institution - known to many, but because of its location elusive to some. It is a very popular lunch-stop, so book a table - there are hourly sittings 12:30pm-3:30pm. Here you can you sample the friendship 'coffee' (grolla), which from its unashamedly alcoholic taste seems unlikely to have passed close to a coffee bean. To ski there, take the narrow, winding red piste from the bottom of the Ruinettes chair, turning left at the signpost to Chez Dany. Follow the itinerary route (and the hundred or so ski tracks before you) through the forest to the small hamlet of Clambin. Beginners or timid intermediates may find the route beyond their ability and the restaurant is only accessible when the snow is plentiful. The crowds congregate here for après - on a sunny day don't expect to get a seat if you arrive after 4pm. A ski-doo is the best option to get there in the evening - ask the restaurant to book one for you - and you can sledge home to Médran. Call to check they are open before you head up the mountain, as if there are no bookings they won't open. And take lots of cash, as no credit cards are accepted.

The building adjacent to the top of the Funispace houses 2 restaurants known as **l'olympique** (t 027 771 2615). Downstairs is self-service with large seating areas inside as well as outside on the south-facing terrace. The food is varied and good, but expensive. Upstairs has waiter service inside and out - the menu offers a selection of tasty salads, pasta, risotto and polenta preceded by a delicious appetiser of brown bread and tapenade. Reservations are essential. When it is sunny, fondue and crêpes are available upstairs on another small terrace.

62 The waiter-service restaurant upstairs at Ruinettes (t 027 771 1979) receives good reviews, whilst the self-service restaurant downstairs is very mediocre and over-priced. A better option for a cheap quick lunch is the **kiosk** lower down the slope, which sells a selection of reasonably priced sandwiches.

au mayen (t 027 771 1894) is a small, rarely busy restaurant the name of which means 'home'. Sadly the service doesn't live up to the name, often being unfriendly and slow, even when there are only a handful of diners, but it is worth going for the excellent croûte - a local dish of bread, cheese and ham. It is also a quiet spot for a restorative hot chocolate with rum before hitting the real après in town.

Halfway down the blue track to Médran the recently erected **1936** marquee is surprisingly cosy despite its tent-like surrounds. When it is sunny skiers spill out onto the snow and as 1936 is the last stop for après on the descent into the resort for many it is start of the evening party.

getting home

The only way to village **on skis** is along the quite narrow but gentle blue path from the bottom of the Mayentzet chair, which winds through the forest. At the end of the day it is reminiscent of the M25 in the rush-hour, not only with skiers and tobogganists flying past at various speeds, but also pedestrians and dogs. Conditions can be poor and in late season or little snow it is often closed. The path starts at Ruinettes, or you can join it lower down by first skiing a red - fast and wide - or a black - fast and often icy - piste, both of which join the blue at the bottom of the Mayentzet chair.

When the path is closed because of poor snow below Ruinettes, you can descend to the village **by lift** - in either of the Médran gondolas.

Lac des Vaux is a minature ski resort in itself, which - thanks to being a sheltered bowl - often seems to escape the worst of the weather. The vertical drop is quite short, but the area offers 1 piste of each colour and the entrance to 2 spectacular high mountain tours. All pistes end at the bottom of the 2 lifts, Lac des Vaux 1 and Lac des Vaux 3, so mixed ability groups can happily ski here together, safe in the knowledge that nobody will get too lost. As the slopes face north-west, the snow conditions stay generally good throughout the season.

access

From the village take either Médran 1 or 2 to Ruinettes and from there either the Funispace or Attelas 2 gondola. Lac des Vaux lies on the left side of the ridge at the top of either of these lifts.

pistes

Lac des Vaux's 1 **blue** piste is a gentle and wide descent reachable from the top of the Funispace - the approach is narrow and busy, so take some care. You can also reach the piste from the top of the Attelas 2 gondola - follow the signs to Lac des Vaux along a narrow path to the left.

The 1 **red** piste is reached by turning right at the top of Lac des Vaux 3 - left takes you to the top of the Tortin itinerary route. Initially it is quite narrow and steep but widens out after about 50 metres. Lower down it crosses the blue

map b

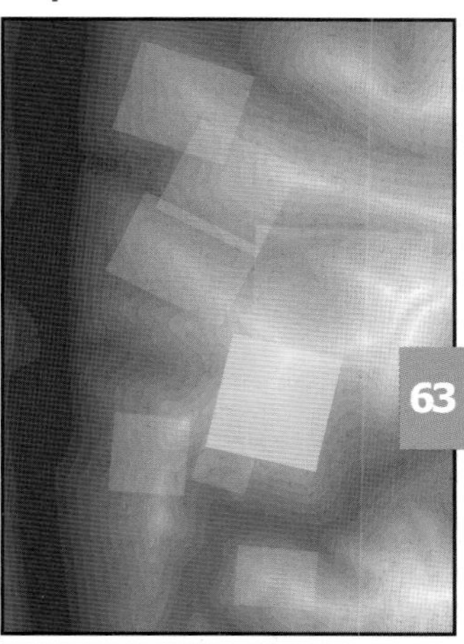

snapshot

out of interest
highest point - 2740m
aspect - nw
lifts - 2 chairs
pistes - one of each, true to their hue
off-piste - 1 itinerary route, 2 high mountain tours & access to numerous off-piste descents
restaurants - 1

highlights & hotspots
vallon d'arbi & col des mines high mountain tours
access to tortin
no chance of getting lost

run, ending at the start of the Lac des Vaux 1 and 3 chairlifts.

The only **black** is really just a tricky red, reached by turning right at the top of Lac des Vaux 1 - ski beneath the Funispace building - or from the top of the Funispace. It splits halfway down - the descent on the right is smooth and fast whilst the descent on the left is shorter but more challenging and often mogulled. A short run, it joins the red piste lower down.

off-piste

From the top of Lac des Vaux 3, you can reach Tortin, Verbier's most infamous **itinerary route** (➡ map c). Spoken of in hallowed terms, this is often the target (and the nemesis) of many a skier's visit to Verbier. From the top you are treated to a vista of a long, steep drop, often with moguls the size of VW Beetles. For many the worst part is making the first turn - but once you're moving the descent is exhilarating. Conditions on Tortin are variable and change every day. As the season progresses or snowfall is infrequent, more and bigger moguls develop. The bottom half is a path, which can be bare in late season or when there has been little snow. To return to Lac des Vaux, take the Chassoure-Tortin gondola.

Lac des Vaux is also the gateway to 2 **high mountain tours**, Vallon d'Arbi and Col des Mines. The main entry to the top of both of these routes is through a gap in the wire fence just above the bottom of the Lac des Vaux 1 chairlift (as you ski down the mountain). The upper part of both tours follows the same route, along a path that hugs the contours of the mountain with a steep drop-off on the right - boarders are unlikely to enjoy the long and undulating traverse. The routes then split at a break in the rocky ridge, as indicated by a yellow board. Vallon d'Arbi is very scenic running down the right side of the mountain through the trees to La Tzoumaz - if you're lucky you may see some chamois. Col des Mines is south-facing and so is particularly avalanche-prone but offers spectacular views over Verbier. It runs down the left (and south facing) side of the mountain coming out at the bottom of Attelas. The entrance to the routes will be closed if TéléVerbier thinks they are unsafe to ski. As elsewhere, respect the signs.

It is possible to access the Creblet and Rock and Roll couloirs from the top of Lac des Vaux. On the other side of the valley, the off-piste route known as Rock Garden (no irony intended) can be reached along a well-skied traverse which starts just below the top of the Lac des Vaux 3 chairlift. A 40 minute walk (at a good pace), some of which is uphill, takes you to the top of the run.

eating & drinking

Unless you stop for a picnic, the only

option is **l'olympique** (➥ attelas) (t 027 771 2615) reached by turning right at the top of Lac des Vaux 1. But a quick drink here at the end of the day can give you enough fuel for the final run down the mountain - or the first drink for a crawl through Attelas' drinking venues.

getting home

Once you are in Lac des Vaux, the only way to return to the top of the ridge between it and Attelas is to take Lac des Vaux 1. From the top of this you can get from the top of the Attelas all the way down to the village **on skis**.

Most people who have spent the day skiing in the 4 Vallées return to Verbier up the Chassoure-Tortin gondola through Lac des Vaux. If it is late and you notice Lac des Vaux 1 is closed as you ski towards it, take the left fork half-way down the red piste along a narrow path (uphill at the end), which takes you to the top of Attelas.

Once you have got to the top of Lac des Vaux 1, beginners, timid intermediates or the very tired can get back down to the village **by lift** - taking the Funispace or Attelas gondola and then either Médran gondola.

La Chaux, similar to Lac des Vaux, is a self-contained area of blue and red pistes making it ideal for beginners, cautious intermediates and children. It is also popular with the ski schools. Towards the end of the season its hills are a good place for a bit of marmotte spotting. As La Chaux has a lower altitude than Lac des Vaux, and as the pistes face south the snow conditions are less consistently good. The top section can be icy in the morning, whilst later on in the season or in the afternoons of warmer days, slushy conditions or bare patches develop more quickly here than elsewhere.

access

You can reach La Chaux from various points on Attelas. Coming from the top the first fork on the left of the red piste down to Attelas (about 1/3 of the way down before you reach the bottom of the Attelas 3 chairlift) takes you down a narrow path to the top of a red pistes into La Chaux. If you are lower down on Attelas, the La Combe 2 chairlift takes you to the top of the ridge between Attelas and La Chaux and the top of the other red run into La Chaux. If you are only as high as Ruinettes you can get to La Chaux on the Fontenay chairlift - reached by skiing along the blue path from Ruinettes. The chair finishes on the ridge between Attelas and La Chaux and the start of one of the blue pistes down into La Chaux.

map b

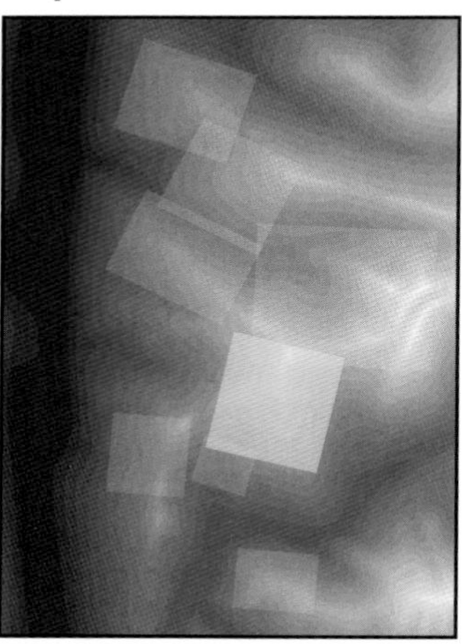

snapshot

out of interest
highest point - 2485m
aspect - s
lifts - 2 chairlifts
pistes - cruisey blues & black tinged reds
off-piste - none
restaurants - 1

highlights & hotspots
the snowpark
some slopes icy in the morning
some slopes slushy in the afternoon
limited range of pistes
good for families and beginners

pistes

There are 2 **blue** pistes. One runs from the top of La Chaux 2 and the other runs from the top of the Fontenay and La Chaux 2 chairlifts along one edge of the Snowpark. Both end at the bottom of La Chaux, and are gentle and wide.

The **reds** into La Chaux are living proof of why the piste colour coding system should only be used as a guide. There are only 2, one reached from the top of La Combe 2 and the other by turning left at the top of La Chaux 2 or at the end of the La Chaux approach path from Attelas. Whilst the lower section of both will pose few problems, negotiating the top of each is more tricky. Both are steep, and sometimes mogulled, with either icy or slushy conditions and rarely anything in between these extremes.

the snowpark

For snowboarders keen to practise some tricks, the attraction of La Chaux is the excellent and well maintained Snowpark, with a variety of jumps, rollers and rails. As you look up the valley you will see a large area on the left side specially reserved for the park. The entrance is under the top of the La Chaux 1 lift, from where a short traverse to the left leads to the initial kickers. Everything in the park has a flag next to it to indicate its difficulty, though you can probably tell just by looking that the little stuff is for beginners, the medium sized stuff is for intermediates, and the big stuff is for experts. The three lines through the park - one for each level - lead to an assortment of hits and the odd rail to grind... and the freestyle slope has a variety of different sized jumps. The snack shack at the bottom sells drinks and BBQ'd food to the accompaniment of a pumping sound system.

off-piste

No off-piste routes start from La Chaux, but quite a large part of the terrain in between the pistes is left ungroomed, and is somewhere to get a taste of gentle off-piste skiing after a dump of powder.

eating & drinking

la chaux (t 027 778 1535) is the only option. Most of the seating is outside - the inside area is small and spartan - so only stop here for lunch on a sunny day. Both quality and choice are pretty standard. For hot food order at the left hatch - and wait for your number to be called - or if you only want drinks, chocolate and cold snacks, queue up at the right-hand hatch.

getting home

Both the chairlifts in La Chaux take you to a point where you get into and down to the village **on skis**. You can't get back to the village **by lift** only - whichever lift you take out of La Chaux, you have to ski at least as far as Ruinettes before you can let a lift do the rest.

At 3330m, Mont Fort is the highest skiable peak in the 4 Vallées. The panorama at the top is quite literally breathtaking - and not just because of the altitude. On a clear, sunny day you can see Mont Blanc and the Matterhorn, as well as the lesser-known but no less spectacular peaks of Rosablanche and Grand Combin. The more immediate view is of a seemingly endless off-piste area where expert skiers descend what look like vertical drops. As this demands superb technique, and shouldn't be attempted without a guide, most people head for Mont Fort's steep black mogul run instead. Ranking a close second to Tortin in terms of infamy, the debate rages as to which is steeper or harder. The whole area is on a glacier so unless you are with a guide - who knows where the crevasses are - stay on the pistes. Because of the glacier and the high altitude, it can be colder up here than in other areas.

access

The most direct route from Verbier is through La Chaux up the Jumbo cable car. If you are on the other side of the mountain at the Tortin mid-station, take the Gentaines cable car. To ski Mont Fort you need a 4 Vallées lift pass - if you don't have one you can buy a Mont Fort extension at the bottom of the Jumbo or Gentianes cable cars.

pistes

red is as easy as it gets up here. And

map c

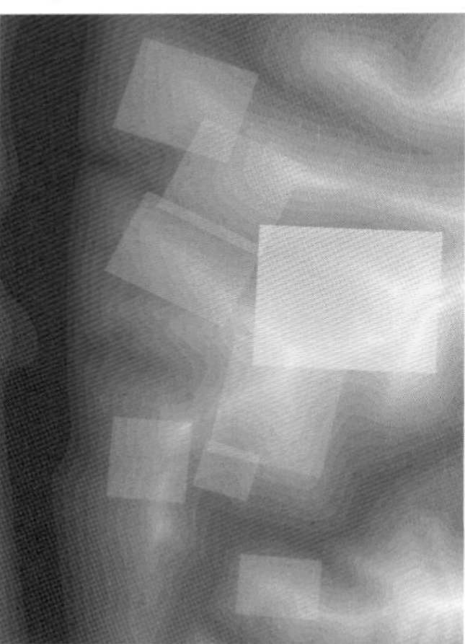

snapshot

out of interest
highest point - 3330m
aspect - sw, w & nw
lifts - 3 cable cars, 3 drags & 1 gondola
pistes - 0 blue, 4 red & 1 black
off-piste - 1 itinerary route
restaurants - 4

highlights & hotspots
the view at the top of mont fort
extensive and easily accessible off-piste
when it's cold it's cold

they are of varying degrees of excitement. The run from the top of the Jumbo down to La Chaux is long, winding and fairly dull - it is a path in all but one short section. Most people only ski it to get back to La Chaux or to Cabane du Mont Fort for lunch. The wide, red pistes from the Glacier draglifts and the top of the Jumbo are more fun and ideal for carving practice.

The steepest **black** in the 4 Vallées starts at the top of the Mont Fort cable car. Once down the steps, you face a sea of moguls. Those at the top tend to be the worst, as skiers fall into the 'follow-the-tracks' trap to get over them, which causes unskiable bumps to form. The lower half is more regularly groomed, making it smoother and faster with one lip from which - if you want - you can get some air.

off-piste

The Gentianes **itinerary route** starts just below the Glacier draglifts. Whichever way you decide to get down will be long and testing and probably mogulled. Less popular than Tortin, the conditions are generally better and the traffic lighter. The lower section is a path which can be bare in spots and for which boarders will need to some speed or a helping hand if they want to avoid a walk. Gentianes ends at the Tortin mid-station where you can take the Chassoure-Tortin gondola to the top of Tortin (➥ lac des vaux) or return to Mont Fort by the Gentaines cable car.

Mont Fort is where the true off-piste kicks off - Stairway to Heaven, Highway, Catwalk, Jacob's Ladder and Backside are all reached from here. However, don't go looking for them without a guide. Mont Fort is flanked by the Bec des Rosses, but you'll probably only see skiers on its steep and rocky sides during the O'Neill Xtreme (➥ events & activities).

eating & drinking

cabane du mont fort (t 027 771 7191) is a very popular lunch-stop perched on an outcrop off the piste down to La Chaux. Inside can feel over-cosy when busy, and the food can take time to arrive. On sunny days, crowds flock to the south-facing terrace causing long queues. Historically a refuge - have a look at the doors in the back wall - you can still stay overnight but you must book (027 778 1384).

Jutting out on a rock under the shadow of Mont Fort, the small **cabane du tortin** (t 027 288 1153) is a short walk from the top of the Glacier draglifts - turn left at the top. Because of its location, it is often undeservedly quieter than worse places - the food served is wholesome and well-priced.

No prizes for food or for service at the **col des gentianes** (t 027 778 1505). The best thing is the large terrace, which is ideally placed for enjoying the sun or for watching the O'Neill Xtreme (➥ events & activities).

la chotte de tortin (t 027 288 1153) is a reasonable self-service restaurant at Tortin. Inside is small and over-warm, and queues can be very long because of the cramped counter system. The seating area outside is large, and is a real sun-trap for a few hours in the middle of the day. Credit cards are accepted for a minimum of CHF20.

Although it is tempting to linger at places like Cabane du Mont Fort, this area is not somewhere to stop for lengthy après - whichever way you intend to return home (through Lac des Vaux or La Chaux) you have to catch a lift. So it's best to get that over with and enjoy a vin chaud in town rather than a long walk home.

getting home

The quickest way down **on skis** is on the red piste to La Chaux, from where you can take either chair back to Attelas. **by lift** the Jumbo takes you as far as La Chaux and then either chair takes you to the top of Attelas. Once there you have to ski to Ruinettes before you can catch another lift.

Also known as 'Super-Nendaz', Siviez is a small, fairly ugly hamlet. Most skiers from Verbier pass through only fleetingly on their way to the skiing around Nendaz and Thyon. Greppon Blanc is the name given to the slopes on the east side of Siviez. Also used mainly as a thoroughfare by skiers to get between Thyon and the rest of the 4 Vallées, the pistes are consequently quieter than those in other areas, and in low season you can have some slopes all to yourself.

The pistes in Greppon Blanc face west and always seem to be blessed with sunshine. Despite this, the snow conditions here are often better than in other areas, perhaps helped by the generally high altitude - most pistes lie above 2200m - and the overall lower volume of skiers.

access

The quickest way from Verbier is through Lac des Vaux, up Lac des Vaux 3 and down Tortin. Once there, take the Tortin chairlift across the flat plateau, coming off at the hut at the top of the blue piste down to Siviez. To use this lift and those that follow you need a 4 Vallées lift pass. The Noveli chairlift, which starts on the other side of the car-park in Siviez, is the link to the Greppon Blanc pistes.

pistes

The only **blue** in this area is the run from Tortin to Siviez. Lower down, it

map d

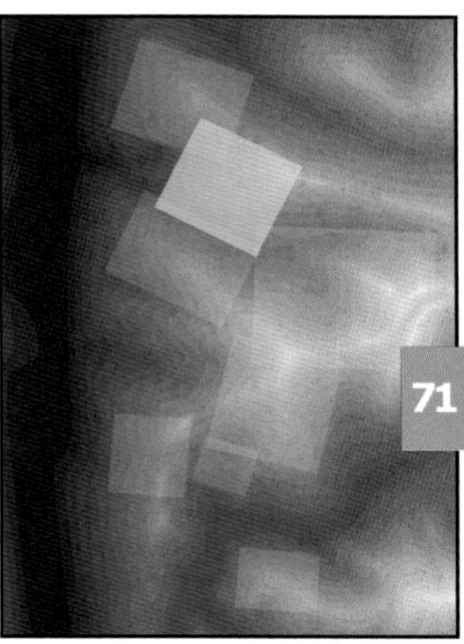

snapshot

out of interest
highest point - 2643m
aspect - w
lifts - 3 chairs & 5 drags
pistes - a long, gentle blue, numerous reds & fun blacks
off-piste - 1 high mountain tour & plenty of pisteside powder
restaurants - 3

highlights & hotspots
the best vin chaud in the valley
chez odette
quiet pistes
numerous draglifts

can be slushy or bare from over-use but when conditions are good it is ideal for beginners and fun for everybody else.

Greppon Blanc takes the **red** run crown with the most varied and exciting collection of any area. The longest of them runs from the top of the Noveli chairlift down to Siviez and is wide and quite speedy. The red from the top of Greppon Blanc 1 starts off as a flat path - annoyingly for boarders, who will end up walking - before sweeping down the mountain. It splits just before the bottom of the Greppon Blanc 3 chair - left to the bottom of the Meina drag or back towards Siviez and right towards Piste de L'Ours and Thyon or the Chottes drag. Intermediates will enjoy these pistes, being wide and long enough to get up decent speed for some carving turns.

There are 2 **blacks**, but if you have just skied Mont Fort's moguls you may question their rating, as neither is as long nor as testing. One runs alongside the Greppon Blanc 2 drag - turn right at the top to reach it - and must be so rated only because it can be icy in the morning. The other starts at the top of Greppon Blanc 3 and is steeper, but shorter.

off-piste

The Eteygeon **high mountain tour** starts a short hike from the top of the Greppon Blanc 3 chair or the Greppon Blanc 1 drag. Amazingly the route ends in the middle of nowhere, but a bus runs reasonably frequently between the end of the tour and Les Masses near Thyon until about 3pm.

eating & drinking

aux chottes (t 079 652 4542) is a large, attractive restaurant halfway down the draglift of the same name. Inside is waiter service and the best table is under the eaves up a small ladder. Outside there are two terraces - the smaller one has the same menu and waiters as inside, whilst the larger one is standard self-service.

chez odette (t 027 288 1982) is the main reason to spend any time in Siviez. Located at the far end of Siviez (beyond the car park and another restaurant) it is an extremely friendly place serving excellent food. All visitors are welcomed with an apéritif - ingredients undisclosed - and fed from a delicious menu of local specialities.

For reasonable self-service **combatzeline** (t 027 288 2041) next to the top of the Noveli chairlift is an option. Its biggest attraction is the sun-baked south-facing terrace.

Après is something you should postpone until after you get back to the pistes above Verbier. But for arguably the best vin chaud in the 4 Vallées, stop at the market stall in Siviez - grab one and keep skiing.

getting home

It's not a short journey **on skis** back to Verbier so reserve some energy. Taking the top of the Chottes drag as the starting point, the way home is along the red piste on the left side of the Meina draglift. Halfway down take the left fork along the track signposted Siviez, which leads to the Greppon Blanc 1 & 2 drags. Take no.2 - you can come off half-way if you're short of time - and ski the red piste down to Siviez. Once there the quickest way home is up the Tortin chairlift, Chassoure-Tortin gondola, through Lac des Vaux and down through Attelas.

The weary won't want to know that you can't return to Verbier **by lift** alone. To get down to Siviez, you have to do some skiing. Once in Siviez, the rest of the journey is by lift - Tortin, Chassoure-Tortin, Lac des Vaux 1, the Funispace and a Médran gondola - except for a little skiing through Lac des Vaux.

Thyon is the furthest resort from Verbier. A modern and characterless place, it is entirely purpose-built to the extent that even the layout of the lifts feels entirely functional, and you'll rarely find a bump on any of the pistes.
The small resorts of Veysonnaz and the prettily-named Mayen de L'Ours ('home of the bear') share the ski area with Thyon, lying at the north end of the valley. The villages are more attractive and the pistes immediately above them are more exciting than those in the rest of the valley.

The runs around Thyon lie between 1800m and 2450m, and because of their generally high aspect, the conditions stay good. There are plenty of snow cannons to keep levels topped up. The villages of Mayen de L'Ours and Veysonnaz lie at 1400m, so despite the snow cannons, conditions can be poor towards the bottom of the runs.

access

The way from Verbier is up through Lac des Vaux, down Tortin to Siviez and up into Greppon Blanc. Once you get as far as the piste down to the Chottes draglift, follow the signs to the Piste de L'Ours, along the path that forks off to the right of the red piste. You need a 4 Vallées lift pass to ski here.

pistes

Too many to mention individually, Thyon's **blues** criss-cross in a spider's web pattern. None of them are

map e

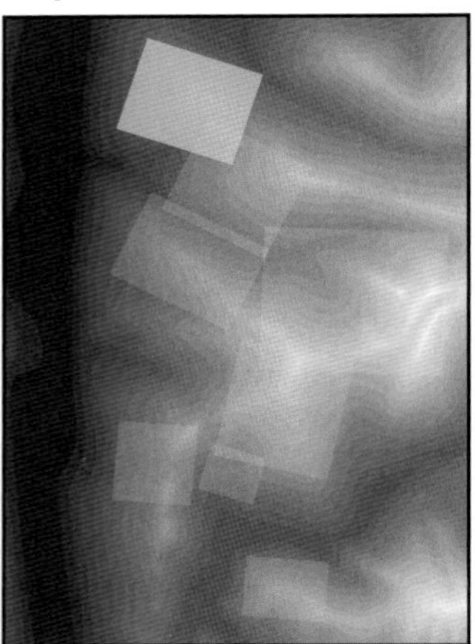

snapshot

out of interest
highest point - 2450m
aspect - n, ne & e
lifts - 5 buttons, 2 gondolas, 3 chairs & 8 drags
pistes - copious blues, almost as many reds & an enjoyable black
off-piste - none
restaurants - several, 1 reviewed

highlights & hotspots
long, racing reds to mayen de l'ours and veysonnaz
a long way from verbier
little for expert skiers

particularly exciting, and most are wide and fairly flat. The main purpose of their layout seems to be convenience rather than fun.

The long, twisting **red** runs down to Mayen de L'Ours and Veysonnaz are the main attraction in this area. Both start just above Thyon and wind their way down through the forest, with sweeping turns and enjoyable rollers. The bottom of the runs are low and can be lightly covered when the snow conditions are poor or the weather is warm. If skied without stopping you will feel like you've had a real workout by the time you reach the bottom. Two other, reasonably fun red pistes run alongside the 2 drags - Cheminée and Les Cretes - whilst another leads to the Tsa drag. A little steeper than the blue pistes in the area, they are also more narrow.

The area's 1 **black** piste runs underneath the Etherolla chairlift and will make you wonder whether Thyon applies a different piste grading system - it's a longish but unchallenging descent.

off-piste

There are no **itinerary routes** or **high mountain tours** in the area, but the piste bashers don't groom all the snow in between the runs if you are looking for some gentle 'off-piste'. Otherwise it is best to head back towards Verbier.

eating & drinking

There are a number of restaurants on the pistes and in the resorts themselves. However, unless you are staying near Thyon or are travelling back to Verbier by road, eating lunch around Thyon may leave you short of time to ski back to Verbier. A better idea is to eat lunch at one of the restaurants in the Greppon Blanc area on your way home.

The **mont rouge** (t 027 281 3195) is probably the only place you should stop for lunch and only because of its location at the bottom of the Cheminée draglift - this takes you to the top of the piste that leads over to the Greppon Blanc area. A long barn-like restaurant, it has a self-service counter serving average food and a small room with waiter service and slightly better and more expensive cuisine.

At the bottom of Piste de L'Ours, you will find an igloo-shaped glass building, creatively named the **igloo**. This is a welcome sight if you skied the piste without stopping and is an ideal refreshment spot where you can sit ouside and admire what you've just come down.

There are 2 restaurants - **remointze** and **les caboulis** - on the long red piste down to Veysonnaz. Both have sun-baked terraces and waiter service.

If you find yourself having après in or around Thyon here you can look forward to adding a taxi ride to your final bill.

getting home

Wherever you have been skiing in the area, the route home **on skis** is the same - take the Cheminée draglift out of Thyon and at the top ski down the red run to the Tsa draglift, which brings you into Greppon Blanc and to the top of the piste leading to the bottom of the Chottes draglift. At the top of this lift, the route home on skis is the same as for Siviez.

If a day on Thyon's slopes has left you too weary to ski home you can only rest your legs once you get to Siviez and the bottom of the Tortin chairlift - from there the journey home can be completed **by lift**.

Nendaz is promoted as an ideal destination for newcomers to skiing, and certainly the runs at the top of the Tracouet gondola are a paradise for beginners and families. However, unless you are staying in Nendaz, skiers with less ability will find the ski from Verbier far less pleasurable or even do-able. On skis, the only way to get to Nendaz from Verbier is down a short itinerary route from Plan du Fou followed by a grotty black run. Although you can descend in the Plan du Fou gondola to miss out the itinerary, skiing the black is unavoidable.

And that is not where Nendaz's problems stop. Another less attractive aspect is the lifts. Some of them have been in place for many years and so feel somewhat antiquated. The conditions are consistently the worst in the 4 Vallées and the snow-making facilities on this side of the mountain are limited so those slopes most exposed to the sun often suffer from poor coverage. The pistes in Nendaz face in a range of directions from east, through north to west and so have a range of conditions.

access

The route to Nendaz from Verbier is the same as for the route to Siviez - up Attelas, through Lac des Vaux, down to Tortin and then Siviez. The link from Siviez is the Siviez chair, which starts just behind the bottom of the Tortin chairlift - at the top of this you need to

map f

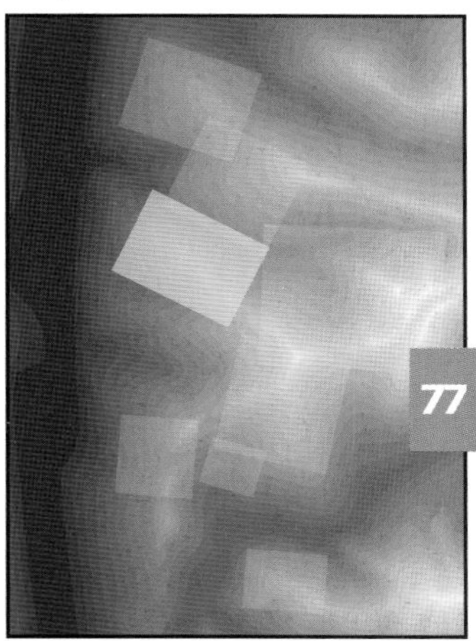

snapshot

out of interest
highest point - 2430m
aspect - e, ne, n & w
lifts - 2 buttons, 1 cable car, 2 chairs, 5 drags & 1 gondola
pistes - plenty of blue, a duo of reds & a nasty black
off-piste - 1 itinerary route
restaurants - 2

highlights & hotspots
consistently poor conditions
few snow-making facilities
quiet upper slopes
access impossible early and late season

take a draglift to reach the ridge between Siviez and Nendaz. A 4 Vallées lift pass is required to use the lifts in this area.

pistes

The pistes around the top of Tracouet are all short and easy **blues**, with lots of space in which to practise and re-practise snowplough turns. For a longer run, you can ski all the way down to Nendaz on a flatish blue piste that passes through the forest. On the way home back to Verbier the piste from the top of the Siviez chair is also a blue and a track in parts.

There are only 2 **reds** in the whole area. One, a reasonably short, unexceptional run, starts from the top of Plan du Fou down the Siviez side to the bottom of the Plan du Fou draglift. The red on the Nendaz side is signifcantly longer - it starts at the top of the Dent button lift and winds all the way down to the town. Conditions towards the bottom can be poor.

The area's 1 **black** run, from the bottom of the Plan du Fou cable car, feels Nendaz's lack of snow-making facilities the most. The conditions here are generally poor, which probably explains its rating. It is not as technically difficult as other blacks in the 4 Vallées, but you need to be confident that your ability will help you avoid the bare spots and rocks that litter the surface throughout the season.

off-piste

The only **itinerary route** in the area is a short, but steep descent from the top of the Plan du Fou cable car. If you've comfortably skied Tortin or Gentianes it will seem like a walk in the park.

eating & drinking

A circular, glass-panelled restaurant, the **plan du fou** (t 027 288 3367) is at the top of Plan du Fou. On a clear day the 360° panorama is stunning. The goulash soup receives plaudits but unless you get there within typical lunch hours you may find little food left or that service has stopped altogether.

Every side of the mountain has one and **tracouet** (t 027 288 2341) is Nendaz's - it looks like and is a functional, atmosphereless self-service restaurant and does not try to beat expectations. But unless you want to ski down to Nendaz it's the only real choice.

getting home

on skis the initial stretch of the descent from the top of Plan du Fou to Siviez is red and then becomes blue. Once in Siviez, there's no more skiing until you reach the top of the Chassoure-Tortin gondola into Lac des Vaux. From there you can ski through Lac des Vaux and Attelas to Verbier.

Unless you take the bus from Nendaz to Siviez - 1 runs every half hour throughout the day - you can't get home **by lift** alone. You can get to the top of Plan du Fou by lift from Tracouet - on the Prarion chairlift, the Fontaines draglift and the Plan du Fou cable car - but once at the top, there is no option but to ski down to Siviez. From Siviez, you can 'lift it' all the way to the top of Lac des Vaux - by the Tortin chairlift and Chassoure-Tortin gondola. Then it's a short ski to the bottom of Lac des Vaux 1, from the top of which you can take a lift all the way home to Verbier - the Funispace followed by a Médran gondola.

A small, self-contained area, the south side of which you can see from the village. Billed as suitable for intermediates and practising beginners, the blue and red pistes seem less difficult overall than similarly graded pistes elsewhere.

Savoleyres is an area with two faces and two types of conditions. The south-facing pistes are most susceptible to the sun, and become barer earlier than the pistes in other areas - at the end of the season you can watch the snowline creep upwards on a daily basis. The conditions on the north side stay better for longer.

access

Verbier's no.1 and no.2 buses go to the Savoleyres lift station. To drive there, follow Route des Creux from the Place Centrale and park in the pay & display on the left side of the station.

The only way up the mountain is in the Savoleyres gondola. Although you can see Savoleyres from the slopes of Attelas you can't ski to it from there.

pistes

Surprisingly given its billing, there are no **blues** from the top of the Savoleyres gondola. The highest one starts at the top of the Taillay chair - the toboggan run to La Tzoumaz starts here too so watch out for tobogganers heading past.

map g

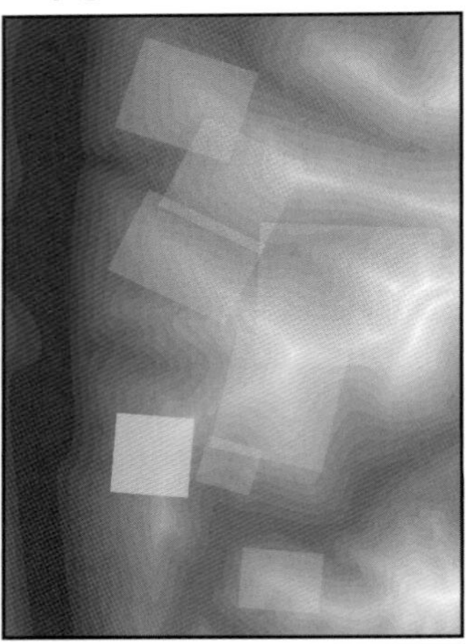

snapshot

out of interest
highest point - 2354m
aspect - n & s
lifts - 5 chairs, 1 drag & 2 gondolas
pistes - gentle blues, a range of reds & (sometimes) 1 black
off-piste - piste-side powder
restaurants - 3

highlights & hotspots
good for all levels of skier
the marmottes restaurants
north-facing slopes get cold in the afternoon
south-facing slopes for all-day sunshine

From the top of the Savoleyres gondola **red** pistes branch off in every direction. On the south face, two wide pistes run down each side of the Savoleyres Sud draglift - the red piste to the left of the lift (as you look down the mountain) is used for competitions and is usually closed to the public. The pistes down to the Tournelle chairlift are also rated red, and are as equally wide and sweeping. On the north side 2 narrower red pistes run down to the Savoleyres Nord lift and eventually on to La Tzoumaz.

The 1 **black** here is not always groomed - running just to the right of the top of the Savoleyres Nord chairlift, it cuts across the steep north slope to join the red pistes down to the bottom of this chair.

off-piste

Savoleyres has no official itinerary routes or high mountain tours. However, you will find large areas of ungroomed, and often mogulled, terrain in between the pistes if you want to practise your off-piste technique or bump skiing without venturing too far.

eating & drinking

Arguably the best restaurant on the mountain, **la marmotte** (t 027 771 6834) has a menu different from the rest in that along with the usual dishes, it offers rösti, served in a variety of ways. Marmotte lies just below the bottom of the Savoleyres Sud drag, so it can be reached on skis - to return to the skiable area you have to brave a lambchop drag. At night, you can reach Marmotte by foot if Route Carrefour is open (a 40 minute walk from Carrefour) or ask the restaurant to pick you up by ski-doo. One way to get home is to sledge down to Médran - particularly sensational when there is a full moon.

For a cosy little lunch-spot **chez simon** (t 027 306 8055), has 2 small seating areas inside, one downstairs and one tucked upstairs under the eaves. The menu is small but offers some tasty options, including a mushroom croûte and the ubiquitous cheese fondue.

The recently renovated **savoleyres** (t 027 771 2116) restaurant now offers a bar, table- and self-service, the takings from which can be enjoyed on the well-placed sun terrace on the south side of the restarant. Food is a reasonable selection of hot and cold offerings, the highlight is the tartiflette, hot from the pan.

The **sky bar** (t 079 449 2916) is a snack bar rather than a restaurant, it only opens on sunny days as nearly all the seating is outside. Serving a small selection of sandwiches, waffles and soup, this is a place to grab a drink and watch the paragliders launching from the mountain.

As half of Savoleyres' slopes face to the south, it is the best area for a piste-side picnic. There are no designated picnic spots, but you should be able to find a comfy enough patch of snow on which to munch your sandwich.

For après there are 2 decent options - on the hill Marmotte is the obvious choice and as the restaurant stays open for evening service, après can become dinner. Lower down Carrefour has a very suitable terrace for a post-skiing vin chaud or beer (➥ attelas).

82

getting home

There is only 1 way get home **on skis** at the end of the day - along Route Carrefour, a narrow path through the forest, which joins the blue piste down to Médran. It passes through an avalanche-prone area and so is often closed - check at the top of the Savoleyres whether it is open.

When Route Carrefour is closed, the only way to get back down to the village is **by lift** in the Savoleyres gondola.

Bruson is the prettiest ski area in the 4 Vallées and has not yet fallen victim to the charm of the tourist dollar. Though development is in the offing for now the chocolate-box chalets on the tree-lined slopes house locals, not holidaymakers. Totally detached from the rest of the skiing, you can't ski there from Verbier, and so is sometimes forgotten, making it a good place to escape to at weekends or during peak weeks when Verbier's pistes become over-crowded. Other draws are the powder bowls and good tree-skiing. With its overall lower altitude - the highest skiable point is 2200m - on bad weather days whilst the rest of the 4 Vallées suffers from high winds and whirling blizzards, Bruson tends to escape the onslaught - the trees making good reference points. Often it is the only area open when weather conditions keep the lifts elsewhere closed. More skiers have realised this recently, so now on snowy days although you will be able to ski, you won't be totally alone. Conversely its lower altitude means that in seasons with poor snowfall, Bruson's lower slopes do not get enough cover and because there is no gondola access the whole area has to close. Most of the slopes face north-east. When fresh snow falls here it stays powdery for longer so Bruson is often still worth a visit even a few days after a snowfall.

access

The only way up the mountain is on the fairly antiquated La Côt chairlift, which

map h

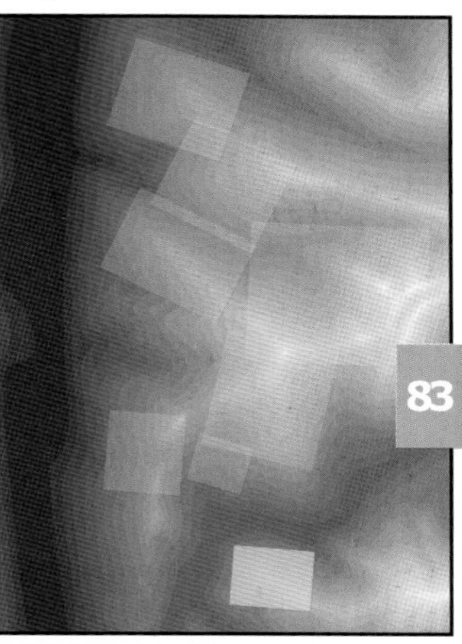

snapshot

out of interest
highest point - 2220m
aspect - ne & sw
lifts - 2 chairs & 2 drags
pistes - tree-lined blues, mid-range reds & 1 speedy black
off-piste - variable itinerary routes & plentiful tree-skiing
restaurants - 2

highlights & hotspots
tree-skiing
no gondola access
perfect powder
often quiet

starts from the car-park. If you need to buy a lift pass for the area there is a small office at the bottom of this lift.

pistes

The highest **blue** is a track from the top of the Pasay chair to the bottom of the Moay drag. It's a pleasant meander through the woods, and unlike other similar tracks is rarely over-crowded. The other blues are also tracks, one to the bottom of Bruson and another to the bottom of Le Châble - conditions on both can be testing.

The most exciting thing about the **reds** at Bruson is the change of scenery.

The 1 **black** piste runs from the top of the Pasay chair. It's a fast descent over a series of lips and rollers.

off-piste

The descent from the top of the Côt chairlift to Le Châble is an **itinerary route**. It is probably graded as such because it is impossible to groom - you are skiing through gardens and over fences - and there is only enough coverage a few days each season.

For skiers who dream of powder, Bruson's is the most perfect, staying fresh and soft for days. And happily, the pistes cover very little of the area, leaving plenty of bowls and open off-piste areas to explore. Skiing through the trees is also great fun if you can rely on your turns happening when you want them to. Plan your route carefully, as the forest hides ravines and steep slopes. Tree-skiing is one instance when a helmet can be a life-saver.

eating & drinking

moay (t 027 776 1946) is a cosy, steamy little place that is as likely to be filled with locals as with skiers. The food is good, and is better value than in other restaurants. Given that you are most likely to be skiing in Bruson when the conditions are less than pleasant, it can seem like an oasis in a snowy desert.

Its only rival is **côt** (t 027 776 1639), a small restaurant serving standard fare. It is rarely busy as it sits on the wrong side of the Côt chairlift, away from the direction of the pistes.

And as you have to catch the bus home anyway, it's easy to linger for après in either of these restaurants - the hours can fly!

getting home

None of the lifts are 2-directional - so once you're up the mountain, the only way down is **on skis**. As you can't get from Verbier to Bruson on skis, equally you can't ski the whole way home. But when there has been exceptional snowfall, you can ski to Le Châble. For most of the season though, the bottom of the Côt chairlift is as far as you'll get, on either a red or a blue piste.

If you get bored of the 4 Vallées, which you'll be hard pushed to become in a week's ski holiday, the small ski areas of Champex, La Fouly, Vichères and Super St. Bernard lie within easy reach of Verbier if you have a car. With a Verbier or 4 Vallées lift pass you need only pay a small supplement to ski at any of these areas.

super st. bernard

Of all the satellite areas, the best known is Super St. Bernard (t 027 787 1110, i espacesupersaintbernard.ch). Affectionately known as 'Big Dog, it shares its name with the huge St. Bernard dogs you see lumbering around throughout Valais. It has operated as a ski station since the mid 1960s.

From Verbier, the journey takes 50 minutes - down through Le Châble, to Sembrancher, where you turn left along the road to the St. Bernard tunnel and Italy. The lift station lies about 7 kms from the village of Bourg St. Pierre, off a turning to the right at the Swiss end of the St. Bernard tunnel. Getting home is the reverse of getting there.

The pistes in Super St. Bernard run from 2800m to 1900m. On the Swiss side there are 2 draglifts from which you can ski a short blue run, a fairly long red, and a black, which often has moguls to rival Tortin's. But the pistes are not the reason most skiers go to Big Dog...for expert skiers, part of Big Dog's attraction is the off-piste. A popular descent is one into Italy, to the small village of Etroubles in the Val d'Aosta, with the promise of a pasta and Chianti lunch at the bottom - just don't forget to bring your passport.

There is a small restaurant next to the bottom of the lowest lift on the Swiss side of the mountain. A fairly utilitarian place with little atmosphere, you can at least fill up on calories before venturing out.

For longer stays, about 6kms from the lift station sits the St. Bernard hospice (t 027 787 1236), which history records as being home to a community of monks for over a thousand years, and a community of St. Bernard dogs for at least a third of that time. A popular stop-over during the summer, in the winter months you can retreat there for a few days if you are willing to brave the elements to reach it - the hospice is not linked by lift and the road is inaccessible during the winter.

So many pistes, so little time. Often it's difficult to know where to start, where to find the longest runs or where to go when there's not much snow or the weather is bad. Here are a few suggestions.

the first morning

Lac des Vaux is an ideal place to find your ski legs. The area is small and self-contained, with short pistes of varying standards. Even the lifts seem more forgiving - with less of a calf-bashing approach than those in other areas. All pistes end at the bottom of the 2 lifts - Lac des Vaux 1 and Lac des Vaux 3 - so if your group splits on the way down, you can meet where the lifts begin.

a long day

The route from Verbier to Thyon covers about 80kms in 1 day and pistes of varying difficulty, so this is for intermediate or advanced skiers only. To get there and back without missing any crucial lift links, and to have enough time to explore the many pistes, you need to make an early start. If you want to spend more time around Thyon without worrying about catching the lifts back, you can return to Verbier by road. Taxi is the quickest option as the journey back by public transport takes hours. The quickest route from Verbier is through Lac des Vaux down Tortin to Siviez and up the Noveli chairlift into Greppon Blanc. The sign to Thyon is easy to miss - where the red pistes split just above the bottom of the Greppon Blanc 3 chair, make sure you take the piste on the right and then a short way down the right fork signposted 'Piste de L'Ours'. The track leads to the Drus drag, which takes you to the top of Thyon, from where you can ski to Mayens de L'Ours, or Veysonnaz, or around Thyon.

When returning to Verbier, it is key to leave yourself enough time. There are often long queues at the Chottes draglift in Greppon Blanc, so you need to allow for them. The essential lift links are the Tortin chairlift from Siviez and the Chassoure-Tortin gondola to the top of Lac des Vaux, so check the times of the last lifts on your way to Thyon. However, once you're in Siviez, you're pretty much home and dry - the lifts are timed to ensure that once you are on the Tortin chairlift up from Siviez, you should make the Chassoure-Tortin gondola. The quickest route home is through Lac des Vaux, but if time (and energy) permits, going via Mont Fort through La Chaux and into Attelas is longer. Lunch is best eaten on your way back through Greppon Blanc.

poor snow conditions

Two things keep the conditions on Mont Fort better for longer than anywhere else: the combined efforts of the glacier and the high altitude keep the overall temperature lower so the snow melts at a slower rate. In fact until recently you could ski on the glacier during the summer. When skiing there in the winter, just don't forget to wear your thermals.

bad weather
As Bruson lies at an overall lower altitude than other areas and is covered by a reasonably dense pine forest, the bad weather never seems quite as bad here. You should still wrap up warm, as all the lifts are uncovered, meaning you're right in the thick of the elements. In bad weather lifts often run as high as Ruinettes but not much higher. But as the tree-line stops just below you're probably happy not to go much higher.

a good lunch
Most of the mountain restaurants in the 4 Vallées are designed to provide sustenance and little else, with a few notable exceptions. Chez Dany just below Ruinettes and Marmotte are old favourites but Chez Odette in Siviez is a little bit special. Odette's does not operate sittings, so you can keep your table as long as you like and peruse the lengthy menu at your leisure. This and the welcome apéritif helps you to feel less like you're on a conveyor belt.

a bumpy ride
If moguls are your thing, Verbier's slopes are normally covered with them by the middle of the season. A good circular tour is down the itinerary routes of Tortin and Gentianes, the black piste at Mont Fort and finally the short itinerary route under the Fontenay chair. To start the day more gently, try the route the other way round - and let it get progressively bumpier.

a mid-week change of pace
If after 3 or 4 days your enthusiasm for steeps and moguls is starting to wane, a day at Savoleyres can provide the perfect antidote. You have to look hard for any bumps, and most of the pistes are wide and gentle. There are great views in both directions: south to the village and down the valley to Grand Combin and north to Nendaz and the Rhone valley. In keeping with a more relaxed day, there are plenty of refreshment stops: the Sky Bar for a mid-morning hot chocolate, Marmotte for a long, leisurely lunch in an authentic setting and a vin chaud at Carrefour at the end of Route Carrefour to round off the day.

après
There is nowhere better up the mountain from where to enjoy the end of the skiing day than Chez Dany situated on the sunny plateau of Clambin. True it's rarely quiet, but Dany's is a dab hand at dealing with the crowds and you never wait long to be served. The only thing to remember is that you've still got a bit of skiing to do before you're home.

For many, off-piste is where the real skiing starts. And Verbier is a good place to look for reality, as testified to by the long snakes of keen boarders and skiers trekking up steep couloirs or making exhausting traverses to find the holy grail.

Verbier's off-piste has 2 personalities. The itinerary routes and high mountain tours are the gentler side - the most famous of which is Tortin - and see skiers and boarders of varying standards skiing or tumbling down them whilst the ungroomed and unmapped back-country is rougher, tougher and makes greater demands on technique.

itinerary routes

Until recently Tortin and Gentianes were groomed and classified as black pistes. Certainly the traffic that uses them each day can make them appear piste-like. They can be skied without a guide, but as conditions are variable they should not be undertaken lightly.

high mountain tours

Generally harder than the itinerary routes, high mountain tours tend to attract fewer visitors. As a result descents can be less obvious, but give you the added challenge of route finding and a greater feeling of getting away from the markers. However, these are both reasons to ski them with a guide.

other off-piste

Whilst none of the off-piste runs are as well known as the Vallée Blanche in nearby Chamonix, the main attraction is that most of them are easily reached from the main lifts and ski area, though you may first need to traverse a slope or ascend a couloir. The effort put in to get there only heightens the experience further, and increases the reward.

Thanks to the 360 degree nature of the 4 Vallées the various off-piste routes face a variety of directions - so on some fresh snow is past its best after a day, while on others there can still be decent powder a few days after a fall. As it would take a whole book to describe the extent of the back-country with justice, the best way to find out more is with a guide. In brief, the starting point for much of the off-piste is Mont Fort - a much asked question is "have you done the backside?", a reference to the steepest side of this peak. Routes from the top can take you as far as Fionnay (a small hamlet a little further down the valley to Le Châble) or in the other direction past the impressive Lac de Cleuson to Siviez. On the south side of Bruson, when conditions permit, you can ski off-piste all the way to Sembrancher or Orsières.

Perhaps contrary to what you might think, intermediate skiers can also find something to suit them. Verbier's off-piste skiing isn't just about vertical drops and narrow couloirs - some routes are gently-sloped bowls with flatteringly do-able descents, the perfect starting place for powder virgins.

preparation

The best way to enjoy the off-piste fully and safely is with a guide. And taking one is more than about just safety. Not only does going with a guide allow you to enjoy the experience without worrying about the safety aspects but it adds value in other ways too. Obviously if you simply want to ski you can just follow them down the hill, but if you have any interest in your surroundings, your guide be will a mine of information. If you want to see a huge crevasse from a safe distance most guides will be more than happy to oblige. Similiarly if there is anything you are uncomfortable with, just ask. If you ski off-piste without a guide you do so at your own risk. You should always take the right equipment with you - an avalanche transceiver, a shovel and a probe - and you should always pay attention to the avalanche and safety signs and warnings. Never go on your own and make sure your insurance covers off-piste skiing.

Wearing the right clothing is essential too. In the high mountain environment, the weather can change from warm sunshine to freezing white-out in a matter of minutes. It can be as cold as -30°C, and sunshine down in town is no guarantee of good weather on the mountain. As you're unlikely to come across a handy store selling extra layers you should take a warm skiing hat, good gloves, goggles as well as sunglasses, an extra fleece - you may need none of this, but better to take it than to leave it keeping your hotel room warm. Though you might not need to pack a lunch, a few snacks (chocolate bars or something similar) and some fluid is also a good idea. Mountain restaurants aren't quite as plentiful once you get away from the groomed and the maintained.

In addition to all that you will need an avalanche pack - including a transceiver, a shovel and a probe. For some off-piste skiing you may also need to take a climbing harness and a rope - your guide will advise you (and probably carry the latter). If you don't know how to use the equipment (and if you don't it's as useful as a chocolate teapot) your guide will show you. And before you go, make sure your insurance covers your adventure.

ski touring

Ever wondered about the seemingly mad bunch of skiers who walk up pistes as well as down? To the uninitiated it can seem a desparate bid to save on the lift pass, or complete disregard for a perfectly good lift system. This 'sport' is known as ski touring or ski mountaineering - the latter is perhaps a more appropriate name, given the climbing up as well as the skiing down and on a 'tour' you travel from 'a' to 'b' in the same way as hiking up mountains in summer. Ski touring means you can get to places not accessed by lift and into off-piste territory otherwise hidden from view. And believe it or not there is immense satisfaction after a physically demanding ascent or descent as well as the enjoyment of being amidst the alpine scenery, away from the mêlée of the pistes.

Obviously, different equipment is necessary. To climb up slopes you need skis with touring bindings, which unlock to allow the heel to come away from the ski as you step upwards. You also carry 'skins' - now artificial but so called because they were originally seal skins - to attach to the base of the skis during a climb to prevent them from slipping down.

The precautions and preparation for off-piste skiing apply equally to touring. And doubly so, if you are planning to stay on the mountain overnight - you will be very far from your nearest Migros, so make sure you have ample provisions. And sufficient clothing - it's hard to get warm once you're cold. This is just one of the reasons to go with a backpack - though if you've never skied with one before you should be aware that it significantly changes your centre of gravity and so until you get used to it you may find your balance is a little off. Also, inform someone of your itinerary and likely time of return.

touring in verbier

If you want to learn the techniques for touring, all of the ski schools offer lessons. Once you have mastered the basics, by far the best - and safest - way to explore further is with a guide. Verbier's off-piste offers many tours for all levels of 'tourers' - there are too many to mention in detail here, except for the impossible to ignore Verbier to Zermatt *haute route* (high level road). As with all off-piste skiing, you should never go alone, always wear an avalanche transceiver and carry a probe and a shovel. Also inform someone of your itinerary and likely time of return.

Ski touring is possible throughout the whole season, but March and April are when it comes into its own, as the weather is more predictable and the days are longer. Consequently guides - and mountain huts if you're planning an overnight trip - get booked up, so you need to plan ahead.

the haute route

The original, classic haute route first skied in the early 20th century, runs between Chamonix and Zermatt. You can join the route from Verbier, going in either direction, although the route to Zermatt is regarded as more stunning and less tiring. The whole tour takes 6 or 7 days and you normally join the classic route on the 3rd or 4th day. It makes real demands on your skiing and your personal fitness, and it should not be undertaken without considerable preparation and a guide. The ski schools often run haute route tours, or you can go with an independent guide or one of the guiding companies based in Verbier. The nights are spent in refuge huts - small buildings dotted around the mountain which provide evening meals, basic sleeping space and an escape from cold and inclement weather. The facilities aren't the height of luxury, but you should be too exhilirated (or exhausted) to mind. Your reward is an exhilirating journey in some of the most beautiful mountain scenery in the world. For a full description of the route see Peter Cliff's book The Haute Route, published by Cordee and available from most bookstores in Verbier.

Verbier isn't a stop on the skiing World Championships timetable - but it hosts plenty of other events during the season. The dates change yearly, so check with the tourist office or on the relevant website.

The events season kicks off with the **24 hour freeride** when skiers race to raise money to benefit the victims of anti-personnel mines. Teams of 4 compete against the clock, attempting to ski the designated route as many times as they can.

Then there isn't much in the calendar until March and the **verbier ride** (i verbierride.com), started in 1999 by Warren Smith. The world's elite free-style skiers meet to show off their skills in 3 disciplines. In the Big Mountain Freeride skiers hurtle down Mont Gelé at break-neck speed. In the Skiercross, groups of 4 skiers compete head-to-head on a specially designed course of slalom gates, banked turns, moguls and rollers. The Big Air allows individuals to wow the crowds with their impressive jumps in the Snowpark at La Chaux.

The **o'neill xtreme by swatch** is a 3 day invitation-only competition of 25 of the world's best male and female boarders and 10 invited skiers. Held on the north face of the Bec des Rosses, marks are awarded for speed, style and difficulty of line. The best spot to watch the death-defying descents is the Col des Gentianes restaurant. Coverage is also shown on the specially installed screens on Rue de Médran, which also show extreme skiing and boarding videos during the event. This compliments the street-party atmosphere that the event brings to the resort - live bands competing for an audience and stalls selling vin chaud and t-shirts.

The end of the season sees 2 smaller events open to amateurs in all disciplines. The first is the **carlsberg high five**, a 5 discipline event consisting a giant slalom, skiercross, boardercross, cross-country and 'triathlon' in one. Anybody who is game can enter. The second is the **verbier challenge cup**, a giant slalom run by the Ski Club of Great Britain. All levels are welcome and you register in the class suitable to your age and ability. For both, more information is displayed on posters around the village.

The **patrouille des glaciers** (i pdg.ch) is an extraordinary glacier patrol race held every 2 years at the end of April. There are 2 categories - 1 of which runs from Zermatt to Verbier. As the name suggests it crosses over numerous glaciers, so competitors must be super-fit and excellent skiers and also competent at crevasse rescue - only for all mountain men and women.

The **ultime session** is, as the name suggests, 1 big party to celebrate the end of the season.

A holiday in the snow is not all down, down, down - here are a few ideas for something else to do on the snow.

If you intend to spend every day of your holiday in Verbier on **cross-country** skis, you will soon get bored. But for a few hours or a day there are 4 routes within easy reach. In Verbier itself, a 5km trail runs from Ruinettes to La Chaux and a 4km trail circles the Verbier Centre Sportif. Further afield, a 20km circular trail starts and ends in Le Châble and a 5 km circular trail runs around Lourtier. A map of the trails is available from the tourist office.

As you are in Switzerland, you can take advantage of **heliskiing** - which is illegal in nearby France. But think hard before you book your first trip, as for many there is no going back to skiing on-piste. Equally don't get too despondent if you don't go when planned - helicopter travel is particularly susceptible to changes in the weather. Heliskiing isn't legal in nearby France, so business booms in Verbier. The most popular destinations are Rosablanche (3314m), Petit Combin (3670m) or on the Trient glacier (3295m). The helicopter lands before you start to ski - much to the disappointment of any would-be action heroes - and you are then led by a guide through snow that is almost guaranteed to be track-free. Maison du Sport and La Fantastique (➥ lessons & guiding) will organise heliskiing (with guides) for you, or you can book directly with Air Glaciers (t 027 329 1415, i air-glaciers.ch)

Maison du Sport organises weekly **night-skiing** at Les Esserts. Aimed mainly at children, it's a short descent on the nursery slope. Despite being apparently easy, the piste is a very different creature at night - see how good your technique is when you can't quite see all the bumps.

On Savoleyres a 10kms **tobogganing** track starts at the top of the Taillay chair down through the forest to Tzoumaz. Tobogganers can also use Route Carrefour, when it is open, from Savoleyres to Carrefour. You can rent toboggans from most ski shops for between CHF8 to CHF15 per day.

For those who can't or don't want to don skis, **snowshoeing** is an excellent way to enjoy the scenery. Equipment has been modernised a bit, but you still effectively wear tennis rackets to tramp around the mountains. You can book a guide through Maison du Sport or La Fantastique (➥ lessons & guiding).

the resort

Cheese, cheese everywhere, and nothing else to eat? Those fearing that the choice will be fondue, fondue or more fondue will be pleasantly surprised. Such is the range of eateries, it's almost impossible to categorise them - pretty much every popular form of cuisine is represented in a variety of settings.

restaurants

No more is the cosmopolitan nature of Verbier more apparent than in its restaraunts. In addition to local dishes and the ubiquitous fondue you can eat sushi, curry, haute cuisine, pizza and burgers. And if you want to eat up the mountain, both Chez Dany (➥ attelas) and La Marmotte (➥ savoleyres) open for dinner if there is sufficient demand. The reviews are split into 'in town' and 'further afield' - for the latter you will need a car or taxi to reach them from the centre of Verbier.

Most of the restaurants reviewed have a small **bar** where you can have a quick drink before dinner. Some of the resort's **hotels** have a restaurant, open to non-residents. Demand for tables is high, so at weekends and during peak weeks **reservations** for evening dining are essential, particularly for larger groups. Most restaurants run 2 **sittings**, 1 at 7pm and 1 at 9pm.

With so many sunny days, most restaurants find space for a **terrace**. As temperatures fall too low for al fresco dining at night they are open only during the day.

snapshot

for something...
at breakfast - offshore
cheap - chez martin
cheesy - le caveau
expensive - roland pierroz
from après to evening - le fer à cheval
late - harold's hamburgers
meaty - el toro negro
naughty but nice - the milk bar
with a view - sonalon

prices

Either because you're dining up a mountain, or simply because it's Switzerland, eating out is not a cheap experience. In the reviews the grading £-£££££ reflects the price per head for a main course excluding drinks.
£ below CHF10
££ CHF10-20
£££ CHF20-30
££££ CHF30-40
£££££ above CHF40
Unless otherwise stated, all reviewed restaurants accept most credit cards.

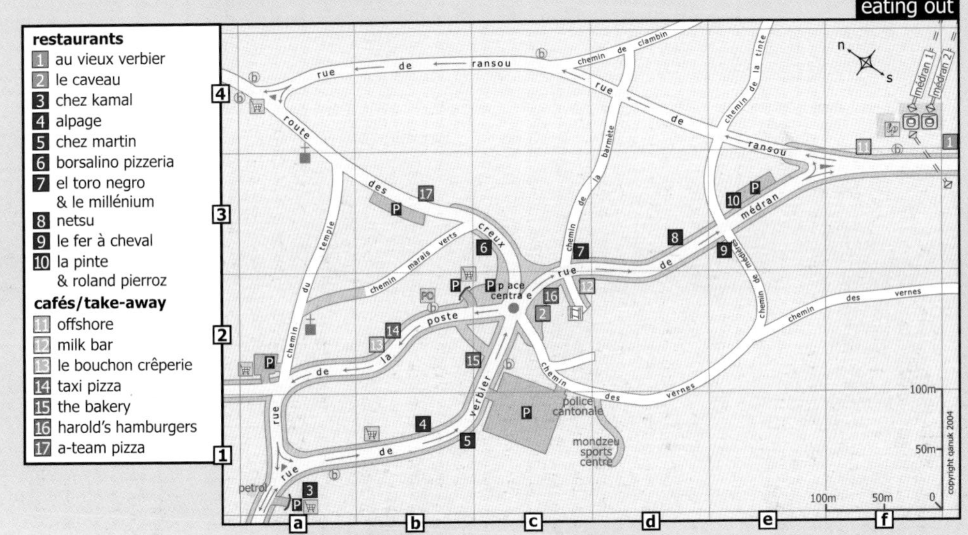
restaurants
1 au vieux verbier
2 le caveau
3 chez kamal
4 alpage
5 chez martin
6 borsalino pizzeria
7 el toro negro & le millénium
8 netsu
9 le fer à cheval
10 la pinte & roland pierroz
cafés/take-away
11 offshore
12 milk bar
13 le bouchon crêperie
14 taxi pizza
15 the bakery
16 harold's hamburgers
17 a-team pizza
rue de ransou
chemin de clambin
chemin de la tinte
chemin de la barmète
route des creux
chemin du temple
chemin marais verts
rue de la poste
rue de verbier
rue de médran
chemin de médières
chemin des vernes
place centrale
police cantonale
mondzeu sports centre
petrol
médran 1
médran 2
n
s
100m
50m
0
copyright qanuk 2004

au vieux verbier £££££

027 771 1668
8am-11:30pm
traditional swiss

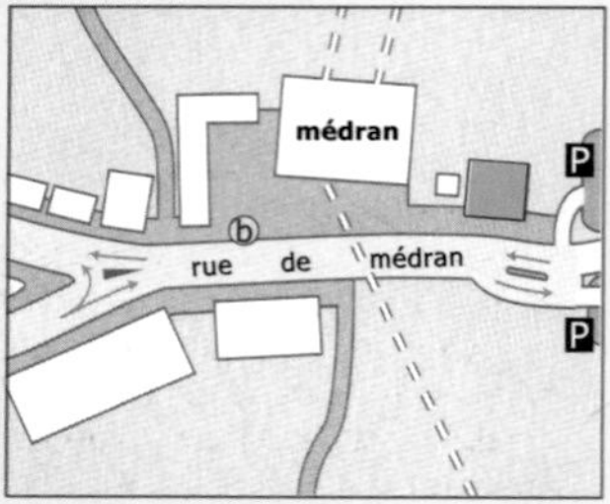

médran
rue de médran
P
P

A deservedly popular venue for lunch, après or dinner, au Vieux Verbier is a large family-run restaurant - the inside seats up to 150 people - which is conveniently located next to the Médran lift station. Despite its size, the traditional alpine interior gives it a special charm, service is genteel and you always receive a warm welcome.

Lunch is served from midday until 3:30pm, and in good weather the spacious terrace - which has room for 100 sun-worshippers - opens to allow you to idle away your afternoon in the sunshine. A special afternoon tea menu of assiettes of meat, cheese and home-made cake is available - or you can opt for something stronger.

The dinner service starts at 7pm but those looking for fondue should look elsewhere - au Vieux Verbier is proud not to serve it. Instead, the house speciality, *La Potence* (the gallows) is highly recommended. Chunks of good-quality beef hung on a spiky metal frame are flambéed at the table and served with a rich bourguignon sauce, rice and tasty French fries. Another house speciality is pan-fried perch from Lake Geneva, which is similarly delicious. Desserts too are traditional fare - rich, filling and hard to resist.

<< in town >>

The place in Verbier for fondue - choose from classic cheese, meat, or tomato served with potatoes. Raclette is also a speciality. Justifiably popular for the delicious food and pleasant atmosphere, on most nights you need to reserve a table, although the earnest maître d' always makes an effort to find space. Those who have had their fill of the local dishes can choose from a wide selection of very generous and tasty salads, spatchcock chicken or steak. If you have room for dessert, the choice is limited to ice-cream and sorbet - but few can manage more.

alpage
£££
p97
b1
027 771 6121
6:30pm-11pm
swiss-italian

Traditional mountain food and style with a modern twist. New in 2003, the Alpage lies on the ground floor of the Hotel Rhodania. Tastefully decorated throughout, pictures of olde Verbiere hang from rough, cream-coloured walls and the wooden furniture is covered with cow-hide throws. On dark, snowy evenings, the candle-lit room feels cosy. Food is rustic and hearty and served in quite generous portions. Service can be erratic, but is always friendly.

The finest Italian job in Verbier. The pizza - baked in a wood-fired oven, with a thin, crispy base and interesting toppings - is the best in the resort, and the homemade pasta and steak is also good. With its bustling but relaxed atmosphere it is a great place for families or large groups, and you don't have to keep an eye on the noise levels. You're unlikely to get a table without a reservation but if you are a small group and there are no tables you may be able to eat at the bar.

chez kamal
££
p97
a1
027 771 7628
11:30am-11pm
indian/indonesian

The only place in Verbier to indulge your craving for chicken tikka masala. Although it doesn't rival most local Tandooris in England, the food at least offers something different. A mixture of Indian and Indonesian - the décor is the same - the menu includes favourites like chicken korma and nasi goreng. A buffet is served on Friday and Saturday evenings - all you can eat for CHF15 from a selection of meat and vegetable dishes, served - of course - with popadoms.

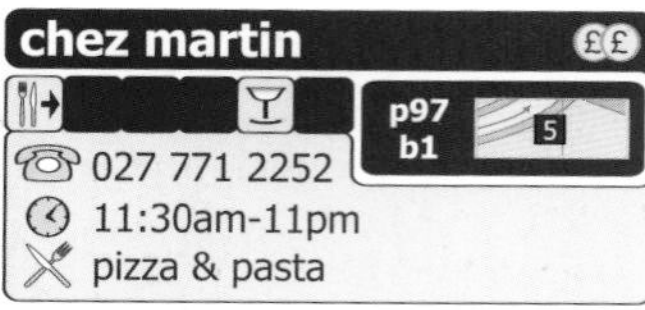

Verbier's cheapest restaurant, Chez Martin serves up standard fare pizza and pasta in a large, fairly bland room, but at very pleasing prices. In particular the lunch menu, available 11:30am-2pm, is good value - 2 courses cost CHF17 and there are 6 set menus. Families and big groups shouldn't struggle to get a table and it's one choice for those searching for food outside normal mealtimes, as it is open all day from 11:30am.

le fer à cheval
£££
p97
e3
9
027 771 2669
9:30am-11:30pm
pizza, pasta & brasserie

Known affectionately as the 'Furry' or the 'Shovel', the giant iron horse-shoe on the roof makes this bar/restaurant hard to miss. Better known for its après in the afternoon, from 7pm the Furry turns into a full-blown restaurant offering pizzas, tasty salads and grilled meats. Whilst the food would disappoint connoisseurs, people love the lively atmosphere and friendly service and it's one of the few places in Verbier where you can order food after 10pm. As it's very popular make sure you book.

el toro negro
££££
p97
c3
7
027 771 9901
6:30pm-11:30pm
steak

Not a restaurant for vegetarians, El Toro Negro's business is in meat: good-quality beef, ostrich or pork. Portions are huge and come with plenty of carbohydrate, so although the extensive salad bar looks - and is - delicious make sure you leave room for your main course. The wine list compliements the food well, with a good range of drinkable reds. Reservations are essential and when you book, clearly state you want a table at El Toro Negro, as the restaurant shares its booking line with Le Millénium. Can be booked for private parties.

The only restaurant in Verbier with a Michelin star - and a price bracket to match. Verbier's king of cuisine, Roland Pierroz, has presided over the cooking at his name-sake restaurant for over 20 years. Food and wine vie for first place, but receive equally careful treatment -

the cellar contains some 50,000 different bottles and the haute cuisine food would compete with that served in top London eateries. With excellent service, it is a good place for a special occasion.

le millénium

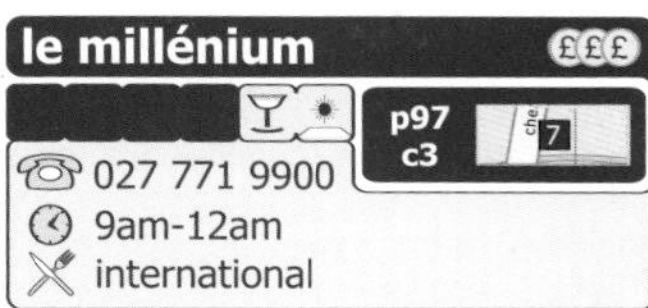

Although Le Millénium has the same owner as El Toro Negro, the choice isn't limited to steak - this is one of the few restaurants to serve a selection of fish, seafood and vegetarian dishes. But you need strong muscles to lift the heavy metal-bound menu, stamina to choose from the seemingly endless selection of dishes and dedication to finish the huge portions.

netsu

£££
p97
d3
8
027 771 6272
6:30pm-11pm (not mondays)
sushi

If something seems wrong about sushi at high altitude in a land-locked country, Netsu makes it right. It's difficult to fault the attention to detail - nothing is missing from the Japanese theme or the well prepared food. You can eat the good, fresh sushi and sashimi at high chairs at the bar - ideal for lone diners - or the more sociable long, black tables and wash it down with sake or just a beer.

snapshot

does it come with chips?
For those who have never tried it (and even those who have), the attraction of a fondue may be difficult to understand - the dish is an artery-blocking blend of cheese (typically gruyère), white wine, garlic and kirsch, in which you dip pieces of nearly stale bread. Dr Atkins wouldn't approve, but it is delicious.

The appeal of raclette, a Valaisian speciaility, is as equally confusing for anybody who watches their health or their calorie intake. A half-moon of Bagnes cheese is heated until the top edge is soft, and the cheese is then scraped off and served with potatoes. Little beats it when the blizzard is raging and skiing is low down on the list of priorities.

It being Switzerland, you might expect rösti (a fried, grated potato cake) to be on every menu. Not so in Verbier - the local cuisine is influenced by French rather than German cooking. Where rösti is served (Marmotte and Carrefour), it is a less dense dish than you find in resorts further east. What you will see on menus is a croûte. Made of layers of bread and cheese, soaked in wine and with layers of ham or mushrooms if you wish, it is then baked in the oven and served piping hot - and is very filling and tasty.

With its ice-laden trolleys of fresh sea-food and bustling, open-fronted kitchen, La Pinte wouldn't look out of place on the Champs Elysées. But once at your table the atmosphere is more typically Swiss. Tablecloths are snow-white, wine glasses twinkle and the service is attentive and friendly. The cooking is supervised by Roland Pierroz, with the result that the food is uncomplicated and excellent - and less pricey than its sister eatery.

<< further afield >>

Tucked away in the forest on the Savoleyres side, Marlenaz is not easy to get to, but is worth the effort. A perfect lunch spot on a sunny day, the terrace faces up the valley with a fantastic view of Grand Combin. During the winter, there is no access by road and the only way there is on foot - a 20 minute walk up the dirt track from Sonalon. The menu offers a tasty selection of local dishes and the day's special is often a good choice.

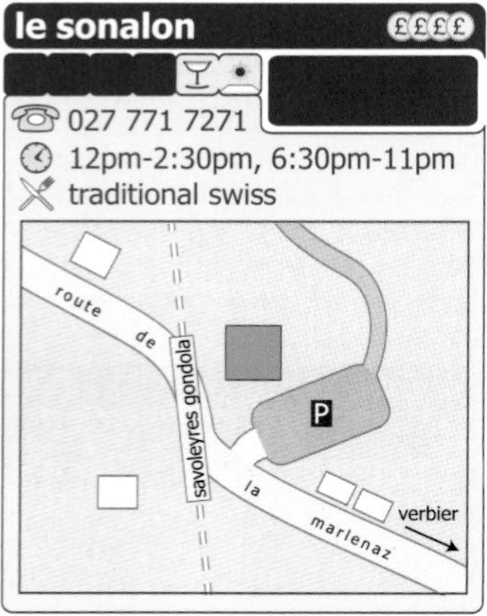

A perennial favourite with locals and visitors alike, Sonalon is deservedly popular for lunch and dinner. Situated on the Savoleyres side, it is closer to the village than Marlenaz - but unless you can face the long uphill walk, the best way there is by car. When the sun shines, the large sun-trap of a terrace is a big attraction. The vast menu will also hold your attention. Sonalon's one drawback? As its sits beneath the Savoleyres gondola, you may feel a twinge of guilt that you are eating lunch rather than whizzing down the slopes.

le carrefour

£££

027 771 7010

10am-10:30pm

traditional swiss

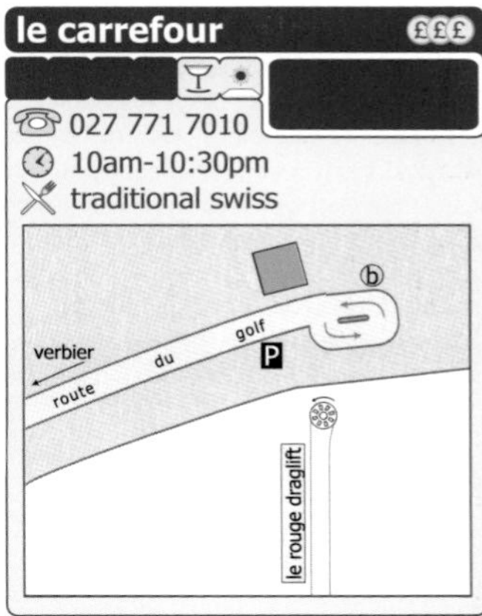

A convenient place for skiers and non-skiers to meet for lunch, Carrefour is located at the top end of bus route no.1 and can be reached from both the Attelas and Savoleyres areas on skis. It is also worth a trip in the evening for a relaxed meal in a traditional setting - if you have a car or can afford a taxi. The house speciality is the 'hot stone' - you cook your choice of meat (beef, pork or ostrich) at your table on a sizzling hot plate. Served with a salad and rösti - the owner's trademark and one of the few places you can get it in Verbier - it is a simple, but delicious meal.

al capone

££

027 771 6774

11:30am-11:30pm

pizza & pasta

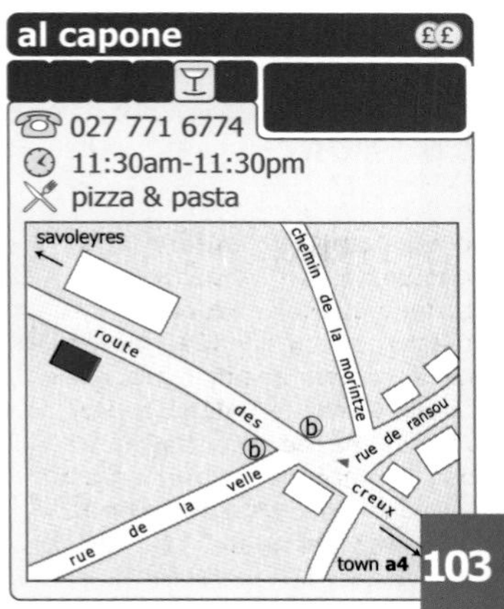

Halfway between the Savoleyres lift station and the Place Centrale along Route des Creux, Al Capone is one of the few restaurants in the heart of Verbier's chalet-land. So if you don't want to wander too far when your chalet girl has her night off, it's a low-key, cheapish place to go with reasonable pizzas and a relaxed atmosphere. As most chalet staff have the same night off, you should make sure you book a table.

cafés

A skiing holiday is the one time you can feel justified in indulging in something highly calorific. As you would expect, the boulangeries dotted around town are filled with tempting tarts and cakes if your sweet tooth needs instant gratification. For treats at a more leisurely pace there are plenty of places to stop. Most of the cafés and tea-rooms open for breakfast, and stay open all day to serve lunch and - of course - afternoon tea. If you pay a visit to Verbier-village, the Marienda tea-room at the back of the Michellod bakery is a good place to stop for refreshment.

milk bar

The Milk Bar does a startlingly good impression of a Cotswold tea-shop, with its chintzy décor, black and white clad waitresses and dark wood furnishings. However, the delicious fresh tarts and cakes are more French pâtisserie than Stow-on-the-Wold. For drinks, the hot chocolate and thick, ice-cream based milkshakes are recommended. With its politely quiet atmosphere it's a comfortable place to spend some time with a newspaper, or to hide from the bad weather when a blizzard howls outside.

le bouchon crêperie

It wouldn't be a ski resort if there wasn't a crêperie - and Le Bouchon on Rue de la Poste is the only one. Previously a Provençal restaurant it has now turned its hand to throwing a good crêpe - you can choose from savoury and sweet filings such as mushrooms, cheese or ham, and chocolate or classic sugar and lemon to eat there or on the move.

offshore

££
p97
f4
11
027 771 5444
8am-7pm
burgers & tex-mex

More inland than offshore, you probably wouldn't expect to find a surf shack in the mountains. Decked out with surf boards, a pink VW Beetle and waikiki prints, it can feel a bit surreal when every inch of your skin is covered in thermal clothing. But Offshore deservedly pulls in the punters for its burgers, tex-mex and ribs. More of a diner than a café, it also serves a brunch menu (until 11.30am) for late-risers who miss breakfast. Service is lethargic, but if you position yourself near one of the TVs showing extreme skiing, boarding and surfing videos, you probably won't notice. The main gripe? Offshore is closed in the evening.

late night & take-away

For some reason most of Verbier's restauranteurs think hunger stops at 10pm. Only 2 places are open for midnight feasters.

harold's hamburgers

Famous for uncommunicative and unfriendly service of which Harold's seems proud - the host displays even less than glowing reviews. Food is average and over-priced, but as Offshore closes at 7pm, Harold's is the only place you can get a burger in the evening. A plus point for some is that you can check your emails while you eat.

the bakery

Got a craving for a midnight kebab? Well, Verbier can't deliver there. However, the bakery on Rue de Verbier has an alternative answer to the late-night munchies. On the way back from the Farm, it's difficult to ignore the aroma from the kitchen, and you will be drawn to a small window where CHF2 rewards you with a pain au chocolat fresh from the oven.

If you are staying in and can't be bothered to cook, a few places will let you take-away. **a team** (t 027 771 3000, open 4:30pm-9pm, delivery 6pm-10:30pm) on Rue des Creux and **pizza taxi** (t 027 771 8844) on Rue de la Poste are both take-away pizza places. Should you only need a snackette you can take-away a pizza slice from Pizza Taxi for a few CHF while the menu at A Team also includes foccacias and alcoholic and soft drinks.

You can also take-away from some of the restaurants - pizza from **borsalino**, **chez martin** or **le fer à cheval**, curry or Indonesian from **chez kamal**, or sushi from **netsu** or **sushi-switzerland**, who deliver (t 079 510 8920) - and it at least means there's no washing-up to do.

For a cheap and quick lunch on the hoof, the choice is more limited. As the supermarkets and bakeries close for their own lunch from 12.30pm to 3pm, you can have sandwiches, or sandwiches. From **offshore** you can get generously stuffed and tasty baguettes with your choice of fillings, or the small **buvette** (t 027 775 3071) next to the TéléVerbier lift pass booth at Médran sells sandwiches and pastries from the Michellod bakery. You can also take-away hot and cold drinks and other snacks.

For those with any energy left, the après-ski and nightlife has something to suit all tastes - an après-ski sharpener, a quiet drink in the pub, or cocktails and dancing later. Apart from a couple of places, the vibe is casual and relaxed. Après-ski is similar to what you find in other resorts - by late afternoon the bars and pubs fill with red-faced skiers seeking to recount the tales of the day over a few beers. Most disappear from 7pm for dinner in their chalets or one of the many restaurants. The nightlife proper kicks off at 10pm and ends as late (or early) as 4am, for those able to stay awake that long.

bars & pubs

Most of the bars are run and staffed by **english**-speaking ex-pats and seasonnaires. Many of the **hotels** have bars, which welcome non-residents as well as guests. Opening times fluctuate, the bar generally staying open until the last drinker leaves. Tuesdays, Thursdays and Sundays are the popular nights out amongst the seasonnaire population, and places like the Pub Mont Fort and Murphy's Bar - and later - Tara's teem with partying chalet staff. On other nights, a lot of the bars can be subdued, unless they are hosting a pub crawl or pub quiz for a UK tour operator. Weekends are busier, when weekenders flood in.

prices

Liquid refreshment doesn't come cheap no matter where you go - a spirit and mixer costs around CHF10, and a cocktail CHF15. Beer is the cheapest at about CHF5 for a half litre. And as anywhere, buying wine by the bottle is more cost effective - as long as you can drink it all.

snapshot

après...
classic après - le fer à cheval
happy hour - pub mont fort
sing-along - hotel farinet

après après...
cocktails - king's bar
happy seasonnaires - pub mont fort
swiss chic - crok no name

& dawn-breakers
beautiful people - the farm
just for fun - tara's

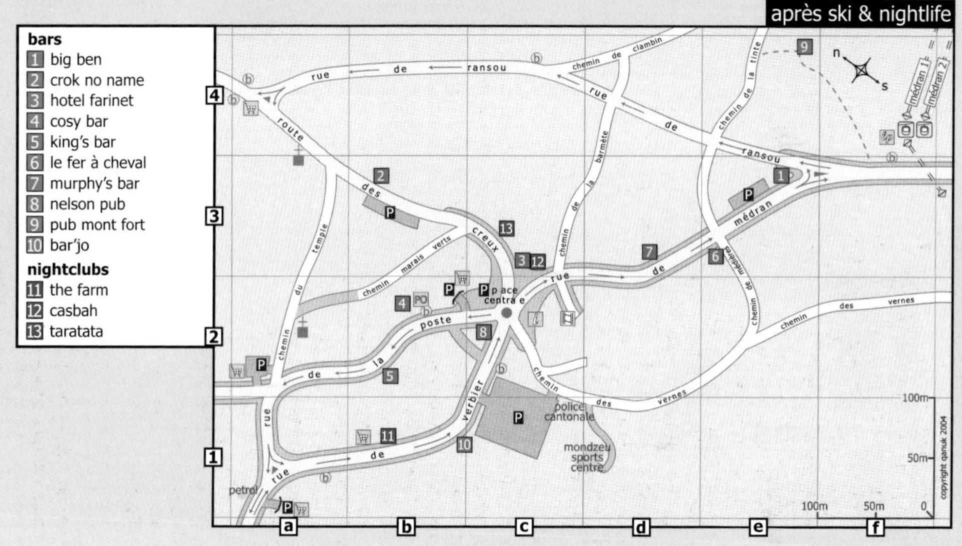

bars
1 big ben
2 crok no name
3 hotel farinet
4 cosy bar
5 king's bar
6 le fer à cheval
7 murphy's bar
8 nelson pub
9 pub mont fort
10 bar'jo
nightclubs
11 the farm
12 casbah
13 taratata
rue de ransou
chemin de clambin
route des creux
chemin du temple
chemin marais verts
chemin de la barmète
chemin de la tinte
rue de médran
chemin de médières
chemin des vernes
rue de la poste
rue de verbier
place centrale
police cantonale
mondzeu sports centre
médran 1
médran 2
petrol
n
s
100m
50m
0
copyright qanuk 2004
a b c d e f
1 2 3 4

crok no name

027 771 6934
6:30pm-1am

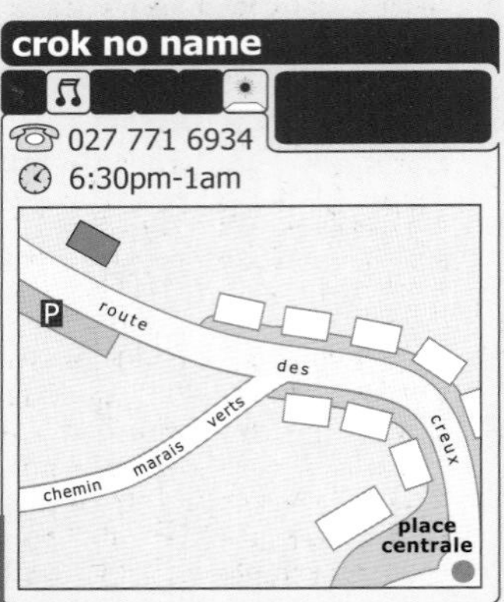

An oasis of calm compared with the other more typical ski resort bars, Crok No Name is unaffectedly chic and cool. The décor is an eclectic mix of styles - the tinfoil-esque ceiling is reminiscent of Buck Rodgers, whilst for seats you can choose between a lipstick-red sofa, a fluffy two-seater, a chair made from antlers or some high-legged metal stools. Somehow, it works, and you could almost be convinced that you are in a bar of a more bohemian part of a European city rather than a ski resort.

Mid-week, the atmosphere can be subdued, perhaps because the prices are too high for most punters. Things rarely get started before 11pm, so even if you want to guarantee yourself a table and seats, you can take your time about getting there. At weekends, the black-clad Geneva set move in pre Farm Club, to enjoy the cocktails and the DJ's choice of Café del Mar inspired tracks.

For drinks, the usual wines and beer are served, but if you want to splash out go for the speciality cocktail - a dangerous blend of long island iced tea and margarita and called a Royal. Expensive, but one should be enough.

big ben

No explanation is given for the name, but no big clocks are visible. Big Ben is popular for après, perhaps because it's the first drinks stop after Médran. You can enjoy the late afternoon rays from one of the benches crowded on the small terrace at the front. In the evening, the crowd is younger, probably attracted by the five pool tables, video games and table football.

hotel farinet

The Farinet could as well be called Jekyll and Hyde. Very much 2 venues in 1, you can opt for riotous fun or relaxed calm. Every day as the slopes empty, the glass-fronted section over-looking the Place Centrale fills up with ski-booted après seekers. Various live bands strum out old favourites to the receptive and enthusiastic audience, who sing along at full volume. The rear part of the bar is more subdued - and more sophisticated. A recent overhaul has given it an excess of comfortable seating and subdued lighting - which lends itself more to cocktail drinking than beer bolting. The bar is still the place to go to watch UK and European football matches, and for the 6 Nations rugby and the Grand National, a bigger screen is set up. You can also enjoy a drink on the terrace beside the hotel entrance.

king's bar

On entering King's, you'll feel you've stumbled across a hidden gem. In reality, it is a well known venue, but it never gets over-busy - the high prices making it somewhere best kept for special or extravagant occasions. The small room has the refined air and appearance of a chic members-only club, but the atmosphere is always laid-back. The cocktail list is satisfying long, with some mouth-wateringly unusual creations, like a grape martini or a passion fruit caiparinhia. But if you're planning to be there for a while, re-mortgage your house first.

cosy bar

The bar in the hotel Phenix certainly lives up to its name and is something of a secret drinking spot - for now at least. Exquisitely furnished and extremely comfortable, the main item on the small menu is wine - much of the selection listed comes from local vineyards but all bottles are well chosen. You can enjoy your glass of Fendant or Dôle while playing chess or just soaking up the chilled out ambience, smug in the knowledge that you were one of the first to find it.

le fer à cheval

A mainstay of the après scene, most visitors make it to the Furry at some point during their stay. A lively venue from mid-afternoon, you need to get ahead of the hordes to be guaranteed one of the prime tables on the terrace - or any of the occasional free pizza that is soon devoured by the masses. If you are planning a long stay a table inside is better, as the terrace soon falls into the shade. Even then, unless you stay for dinner, après ends when the restaurant starts its service at 7pm. Any ski instructor stalkers should start here - the Furry is a favourite watering-hole of many a Jean-Noël and Edouard you might have admired on the slopes.

murphy's bar

Murphy's Bar on the ground floor of Hotel Garbo suffers from something of an identity crisis. It aims for sophistication with a tempting cocktail menu, but the inside resembles an empty warehouse. The void doesn't matter when the bar is busy, but when quiet it can feel cavernous and empty. Cocktail orders can be greeted with derision or confusion, so get to know your bar staff before parting with CHF15 for a quickly-drunk mojito. Après here can be subdued, except on sunny days when people gravitate to the palm-tree-decked terrace on the roof of the bar, which is open from 2pm until sunset. The inside bar is more of a late evening venue, and fills up from 10pm onwards. Lively theme nights are a regular event here - mardi gras especially should not be missed.

pub mont fort

Something of a Marmite bar, you'll either love it or hate it here. Busy, young and in need of a face-lift, Le Pub is inexplicably popular. When the sun shines, the large terrace fills with seasonnaires making the most of Verbier's only happy hour (4pm-5pm). After 5pm, drinks double in price - so buy your round before then or make the most of one of the regular drinks promotions. Better still, befriend a seasonnaire, as they get discounted drinks all night, which is presumably why an above average quota of chalet girls and boys, reps and plongeurs drink here. After the mid-evening lull, the 2 floors fill up again - downstairs tends to be more chilled out. During the early evening hours it is the En Bas restaurant (for reservations t 027 771 1834), although eating gives way to shooting (shots) later on. Le Pub holds regular theme nights, but don't expect to get in if you're not '[in theme'. If you want to check your email, there is an internet terminal in a small alcove off the main bar.

wonderbar

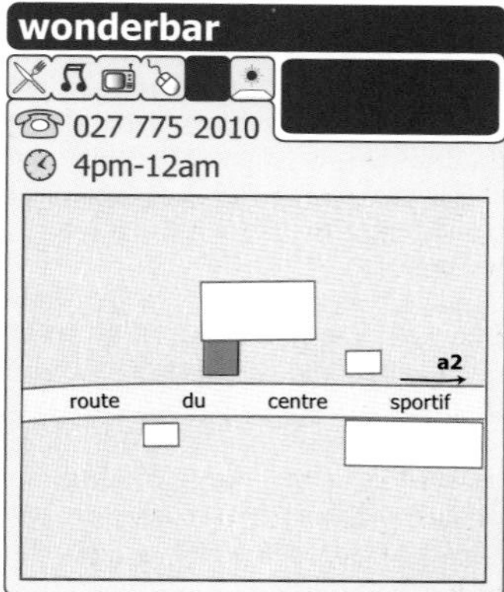

A welcome addition to the western end of the resort, the Wonderbar on Rue du Centre Sportif brings new life to an otherwise quiet quarter. Knowing that its main market will be the hordes of season workers who live nearby, the bar caters for them accordingly - delivering fun and lively après in a similar way to the Pub Mont Fort above Médran. The choice of entertainment is very much yours - pool, darts, pinball, internet surfing, live music, drinks promotions... though of course you can just order a pint and enjoy it with your mates. Bar snacks are also on offer for the peckish, and sports events are regularly screened for football or rugby fans. On bad weather days the bar opens at midday.

nelson pub

For the home-sick few, the Nelson is the best medicine in Verbier. Truly resembling a traditional English pub, inside is all dark wood furniture, chintzy wallpaper and a smoky atmosphere. The picture is completed by a darts board and a pool table. Situated just off the Place Centrale, gamblers will be keen to know that it also houses Verbier's only betting shop.

bar'jo

Bar'jo is Crok's main competitor. A subterranean venue, underneath Chez Martin, from the outside there are few clues as to what is going on behind the front door. It's a case of taking your chances - and normally the outcome is good. The atmosphere is invariably laid back and cool and the background music less cheesy and mainstream than that played elsewhere.

nightclubs

All of the bars are closed by 1:30am, but the nightclubs are open to 4am to entertain those not so keen to catch the first lift. Nightclubs in ski resorts are often an interesting phenomen, and often seem to be the place where bad records go when they retire. Fortunately Verbier's clubs understand slightly better what their clientele want to dance to and play a little less unrecognisable German techno than you might hear else where. All the clubs reviewed are open 7 nights a week.

At weekends and on busier evenings, the more **girls** in your group, the quicker you will get in, just like any club in the world. None of the clubs have a **dress** policy, so there's no need to dig out the glad rags - you'll get in even in jeans and outdoor boots.

prices

No surprises - drinks are expensive. Spirits can be bought by the bottle and mixers are then provided free - if you are part of a group - or will go back most nights - this works out as fairly good value. If you don't finish your bottle in one sitting, the bar will hold it for you until you finish it, even if it takes all season. Cover charges vary from place to place - only the Farm doesn't have one - and also what time you arrive. Cloakrooms also levy a minimal fee.

Verbier's most infamous nightclub is best for star-gazers and celebrity spotters - Fergie was a regular when she worked in Verbier as a chalet girl. Now, the Farm still attracts an affluent crowd, happy to spend CHF200 on a bottle of spirits, so it's a great place to people-watch. Make sure you get there before 11:30pm on Fridays and Saturdays just to get in - and even if you reserve a table, you shouldn't expect more than one by the door if you're a Farm virgin. The door policy is a bit hit and miss - you're greeted like a long lost friend on the quieter week nights, and given something of the cold shoulder at weekends. But this cool treatment doesn't deter the ever-eager crowds jostling for position at the door - when standing in line, it helps to look lovely and loaded and that you intend to part with your cash.

taratata
p107
c3
13
027 771 4535
11:30pm-4am

Underneath the Hotel Bristol and known more commonly as Tara's, the clientele is younger and hipper than at the Farm and the attitude is more about having fun than being the most beautiful. The music seems to be selected by its danceability rating, which helps keep the dance-floor well populated. As with the Farm, the door policy can be unfriendly when they don't need your business, but welcoming when they do. Tara's has a proactive approach to upping its girl ratio, often letting girls in for free after 1:30am or on certain nights of the week.

casbah

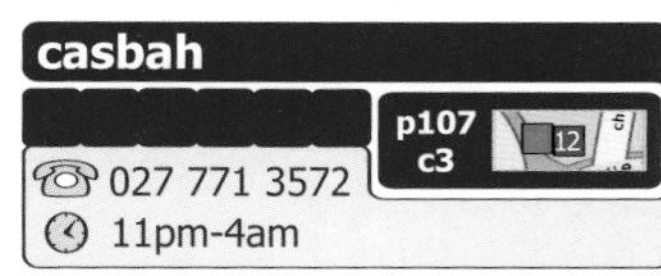

027 771 3572
11pm-4am

The newest addition to the Verbier club scene and the least ski resort-like in nature. Housed in the basement of the Hotel Farinet (in place of Marshals, the boarders' favourite) the Casbah is a haven of North African styling with whitewashed walls and curios seemingly plucked from a Moroccan bazaar - though anybody who is a regular at a Fez Club or the now defunct Po Na Na chain of clubs will feel immediately at home. The result is a fairly laid back ambience - and if you get one of the leather-covered seats you may be reluctant to move. Drinks are more familiar than the décor - as are the prices which are typical nightclub. The music too should ring some bells - it is normally a mix of chart hits, popular dance and r&b, which soon gets the dancefloor buzzing.

snapshot

what to drink...
France, Spain, and New Zealand - all countries you associate with fine wine. But Switzerland? Not somewhere that immediately springs to mind, but either the altitude or the holiday-spirit make the local Valais wine quite drinkable. Fendant is a light, crisp, dry white whilst Dôle is a fruity red, a blend of Pinot Noir and Gamay grapes. Or the Dôle Blanche is an enjoyable rosé. If you want something warm there is always vin chaud - a combination of hot red wine brewed with spices.

Beer also doesn't seem very Swiss, but they must have taken tips from their neighbours, as the national ales such as Cardinal aren't bad. You can buy better known lagers for slightly more CHF. For something different, try the cloudy German weissbier, or a panaché (lager shandy) for refreshment - it doesn't carry the stigma it does in the UK.

For those with steel-lined stomachs or a masochistic appetite, the local fire-water is Willamine (a pear-based schnapps). Some restaurants offer a shot of this or something equally evil on the house, to round off your meal - perhaps the generous nature of the Swiss... or simply the restaurant trying to get rid of you?

When the lifts are closed because of too little - or more frustratingly - too much snow, or your muscles just can't take any more, the resort and surrounding area offer a few attractions to keep you occupied.

more exercise?

The Verbier **centre sportif** (t 027 771 6601, i verbier-sports.ch) is a large complex just off Rue du Centre Sportif - just look for the unmissable hexagonal-shaped roof. The facilities are extensive - a 12mx25m indoor heated pool, a 30mx60m indoor ice-rink, tennis and squash courts, a sauna, Turkish bath and solarium suite, a curling rink and an indoor climbing wall. Open 10am-9pm every day, you can pay as you go - how much you pay depends upon what you want to do - or buy a 7 day holiday pass. You can also swim at the **mondzeu swimming pool** (t 027 771 4158) - smaller than the Centre Sportif, generally quieter and more centrally located - only a 2 minute walk from the Place Centrale. Facilities include an indoor heated pool (10x20m) and a sauna and a fitness centre. It is open daily (except Wednesdays) 10am-12pm and 3pm-8pm. You can pay as you go or buy a book of tickets at a reduced price, good for 3 visits.

With over 20 ice cascades in the Val de Bagnes area during the winter months, **ice climbing** is a popular sport. The uninitiated first climb an artifical pyramid before progressing to the frozen waterfalls. Instruction can be booked through any of the ski schools.

Golfers worried about keeping their handicap can keep their swing going at the **indoor golf centre** (t 027 771 6108). Located on Rue de Ransou it has a driving range, a simulator, a swing analysis and a putting green.

take to the skies

You can't fail to notice the colourful parachutes of **parapenters** circling overhead the slopes on a sunny day. One-off flights - normally for an hour - and short courses can be booked through Centre de Parapente (t 027 771 6818, i flyverbier.ch - or through the Maison du Sport), L'Envol (t 079 679 9452) and Max Biplace (t 027 771 5555/079 219 3655 - or through La Fantastique). On average, a hour's flight costs CHF170. For real enthusiasts Verbier Summits (t 027 776 1134, i verbiersummits.com), run by the charming Belbas twins, offers flying holidays which include accommodation and parapenting courses.

chill out

For somewhere to ease away your aches and pains try the Martine Michellod Massage and Therapy centre, a **sauna**, **massage** and **hammam** complex behind the Post Office (t 027 771 7180). All of the beauty salons offer massages as well as varying ranges of beauty treatments - try any of Ambrosia (t 079 332 4430/027 771 2177), Artemis (t 027 771 2158), Océane (t 027 771 6170), A Fleur de Peau (t 079 611 2826) - though the Spa by Valmont (t 027 771 3450) on Rue de la Poste is the most luxurious option. And to find inner calm you can join the weekly **yoga** classes held at the white church - details from Ambrosia.

culture vulture

Verbier's small, theatre-like **cinema** (t 027 771 2435) shows mainstream English and American blockbusters and some French films. Each film is shown twice a day for 2 days, normally at 6pm or 6:30pm and again at 8:30pm or 9pm. See the fortnightly leaflet for details of the screenings. Entrance is CHF15-22.

If you're interested in alpine history, the **museum** at Le Hameau (t 027 771 7560, i lehameau.ch) is worth a visit for its displays on Alpine history and civilisation. The museum is based just beyond the nursery slope at Les Esserts and opens Tuesdays-Fridays 10am-12pm and 1:30pm-6pm. For art-lovers, the **galerie d'art la foret** (t 027 771 8700) at Le Hameau opens Mondays 10am-12pm, Thursday to Saturday 10am-12pm and 4pm-7pm.

escape the cabin fever

If the sometimes claustraphobic atmosphere of the resort gets too much, trips to Lavey les Bains and Martigny are doable within a day.

Unsurprisingly for an area known for its spring water, thermal spas are in abundance and the baths at **lavey les bains** (t 024 486 1555, i lavey-les-bains.ch) (just off the A9) are the best. Originally built to treat patients suffering from a range of ailments, now most people just go there to relax. Set underneath an imposing face of rock, the complex has a huge outdoor pool with water jets and whirlpools, all at comfortably warm temperatures (30°C - 36°C). Open daily 9am-9pm, you can also enjoy the indoor pool, hammams and saunas.

The oldest town in the canton is **martigny**, which sits on the banks of the Rhône river. Some buildings date back to Roman times, including the striking Bâtiaz Castle, which you can see as you approach the town on the motorway from Geneva. Now, it is a pleasant market town, with tree-lined streets and a mixture of high-street shops and quirky boutiques. Away from the shopping the big attractions include the ampitheatre and the Fondation Pierre Gianadda, which has regular art exhibitions and musical concerts. Towards the end of the season, the *combats des reines* (cow fights) are held in Martigny and throughout Valais. Historically held so the local cows could battle out who got to lead the herd up the hill to the summer pasture, now the emphasis is more on breeding the 'queen' of the herd and on having a good time.

Compared to family friendly areas such as the 3 Vallées, the facilities in Verbier for children are more limited. Few of the tour operators offer the kids clubs and childcare available elsewhere and the resort itself is not amazingly equipped - perhaps because Verbier is not strongly promoted as a destination for families. Below is a summary of the childcare and ski school options and other activities offered.

tour operators

Many of the UK operators offer discounted or free child places in their chalets and will provide a special meal for children in the evenings. Some also include free ski and boot hire, lift passes or ski lessons for childen in their packages. However, only **simply ski** offers a childcare programme - otherwise you have to rely on the resort's kindergarten and crêche facilities. If you book the whole of one of Simply Ski's chalets, they will provide a private nanny service - for children aged 6 months to 8 years, up to a maximum of 3 children. The more up-market operators can generally organise babysitters on an ad hoc basis for an additional fee. Whichever operator you book with, make sure to request a cot or high-chair if you need one.

in-resort

For short-term childcare, the tourist office keeps a list of registered **babysitters** - expect to pay CHF15-25 per hour. Another option is one of the hundreds of English-speaking seasonnaires who are happy to earn a few extra CHF.

Les Schtroumpfs (t 027 771 6585) is a non-skiing **kindergarten/crêche** based by Les Moulins ski slope and run by Brigitte Tisseres. The crêche will take children aged 3 months-4 years and all staff are qualified carers. The centre is open Mondays-Saturdays 8:30am-5:30pm and 9:30am-5:30pm on Sundays. You can leave your child for a full day - lunch is provided - or a half-day (8:30am-11:30am or 1:30pm-5:30pm). Book ahead as the crêche can only accept a limited number of children and remember your child's medical vaccination certificates.

Maison du Sport, La Fantastique, Altitude and European Snowsport (➥ lessons & guiding) run group **ski lessons** for children (from as young as 3 years up to 12, depending upon the school) Mondays-Fridays. Children must wear a helmet to join a group lesson. Make sure it fits well - childrens' heads don't grow as quickly as their bodies, so they should be able to use it for a couple of years. You can buy an animal cover to make it more appealing. The cost of lessons does not include a lift pass. As the majority of them take place on the main pistes, all children whatever their age must have one (➥ lift passes).

Younger children (aged 3-6 years) can take ski lessons at the Maison du Sport Kids Club (t 027 775 3363) - learning to ski is the main activity at the Club, which is open Mondays-Saturdays, 8:30am-5pm. Based in a specially-designed garden at Les Moulins, it is a safer and less threatening place to learn than the main pistes, with a gentle ski slope, escalator and baby-lift. You can leave your child for a full or half-day (8:30am-11:15am or 1:30pm-5pm) and lunch is available.

If your kid is keen on skiing but you would rather be on a beach, Les Elfes international children's camp (t 027 775 3590, i leselfes.com) may provide the solution. Aimed at children aged 8-22 years, accommodation is provided in 1 of 2 specially designed chalets - linked by a tunnel. During the day children learn to ski or board with trained instructors - many of whom are English. After skiing and in the evening other activities - such as squash, swimming and sledging - are organised. Language classes in English, German or French are an optional extra.

Elsewhere in the resort **activities** are organised for children during the season. On the snow, the Maison du Sport run night-skiing once or twice a week at Les Esserts and a torchlit descent from Les Ruinettes every Wednesday evening. A small supper is served first at Les Ruinettes, and then at about 6pm the children ski down accompanied by Maison du Sport instructors. After the day's skiing, *Le Sentier Suspendu* (the Suspended Walkway) is a fun activity for children and adults alike. A series of ropes, walkways and bridges hang from trees in the forest just past Médran. A harness and a helmet are provided, and you are accompanied by a guide. There is also a 4-faced climbing tower. Book through the Maison du Sport. Children must be taller than 120cm. Special events are also organised at festive periods - including the arrival of Father Christmas, fancy dress at Mardi Gras and an Easter egg hunt.

Off the snow, the cinema shows a film for children at 5pm. When the weather is bad enough to close most of the lifts, an extra screening is shown, normally at 3pm or 3:30pm. For would-be disco-queens Tara's nightclub organises a children's afternoon for 7-13 year olds every other Sunday.

Most of Verbier's restaurants and cafés welcome children - the friendliest are **borsalino**, **chez martin** and **offshore** (➞ eating out) - and some offer a childrens menu. Children are generally allowed into the bars and pubs and it is up to you whether they drink - generally nobody bats an eyelid if a child or teenager drinks wine with their parents.

before you go

Before you decide what kind of job you want you need to decide what kind of season you want - a job as a rep will be better paid but you have more responsibility, while a job as a chalet host means fixed hours, but once you know the routine, more time to make the most of resort life. Most of the UK ski companies recruit seasonal workers - interviewing normally starts in May, though there may still be vacancies as late as December. Either contact the companies directly (not forgetting smaller or overseas based ones) or go through a recruitment website such as **natives.co.uk** - who have a comprehensive database of available jobs as well as a lot of information on everything about "doing a season" - **findaskijob.com** or **snowsportrecruitment.com**. It's a competitive market for jobs and while it is not essential, speaking reasonable German will help.

If you haven't got a job by October, it's worth going to the Ski Show at Olympia - some tour operators have a stall there as do Natives. If you haven't got a job by the start of the season, it can be worth heading out to the resort (if you can support yourself for a bit). Some of the less glamourous jobs may still be available and you will also get known - so when there is the inevitable fall-out of recruits due to unsuitability, New Year flu and mid-season blues, you can step into the role. Jobs constantly become available throughout the season - the ski market is very transient.

Once employed most companies organise your **work permit**, **travel** to and from the resort, **accommodation**, **lift pass** and **equipment rental**. Most seasonnaire jobs come with a shared room as part of the package. If accommodation doesn't come with your job - or if you aren't planning on having a job - you would be well advised to find some digs before you head out. Accommodation in Verbier is notoriously difficult to find and you need to start looking as early as the summer - the tourist office releases a list of available apartments in July. Prices too are rising so some seasonnaires are opting to live down the valley in Le Châble. To work legally in Switzerland, you must have a work permit. The rules change on a regular basis - presently the permit is applied for by the employer but belongs to the employee, valid for employment anywhere in Switzerland, for any company for the length of its validity.

once you're there

Most seasonal workers in Verbier are English, with some representatives from Scandinavia and the Antipodes. The seasonnaire population is not particularly big (if compared to Chamonix) nor particularly small (if compared to Zermatt) though it has more than its fair share of long-timers and seasonnaires who don't need to get a job. It is a fairly friendly community though cliques do form - especially among nationalities and companies. That said, season workers in Verbier tend to fall into one of 2 categories - those who go to ski and those who go to drink - so you should find a home somewhere. There are few **happy hours** and for seasonal workers it is one of the more stingy resorts - only the Pub Mont Fort and the Wonderbar offer price reductions for seasonnaires. There is a distinct weekly pattern to the nightlife - perhaps more so than in any other resort. Sundays, Tuesdays and Thursdays are the popular nights out and if you head to one of the bars in favour - typically the Pub Mont Fort, Murphy's and the Wonderbar - you can normally find somewhere lively. For après the Pub and the Furry are popular and during the day Offshore provides a haven from the cold. There are plenty of parties to crash throughout the season - particularly during December and early January when the resort plays host to the British Army - and many of the bars hold theme nights which are seasonnaire dominated.

Verbier has pretty much everything you need - laundries, supermarkets, dvds to rent, and even a library should you be taking the winter off to catch up on your reading. If you have good intentions to learn something while you're there - and capitalise on it early on before they disappear in a haze of Dôle Blanche - you can take lessons in swimming and climbing at the Centre Sportif. There are also a number of language teachers if you are looking to improve your French. For the last couple of years BASI has run a foundation course and a level 3 instructor course in Verbier - perfect for any wannabe instructors. It is also relatively easy to get work experience as an instructor or do some shadowing with one of the English-run ski schools.

Calls home are expensive from an English **mobile**, so it could be worth investing in a Swiss SIM card and calls made within and out of Switzerland will be cheaper and you won't pay to receive calls from the UK. Check that your phone is 'unlocked' (so you can insert a foreign SIM card into it) before you leave the UK. You then pay as you go as you would in the UK. Top up cards are available from the Navilles in the resort. Orange is the best network for international calls, as it charges by the second rather than the minute. There are plenty of **internet** points - the cheapest is at the Centre Sportif, though Harold's has the most terminals and wifi connection if you packed your own laptop. For full details of what's going on in and around the resort, you can tune in to Rhone FM between 7am-9am for information on the ski area (lifts, pistes and weather reports) and events in and around the town. For less official news there's always the seasonnaire grapevine.

the a-z

tour operators

A list of the English based tour operators offering a range of accommodation in Verbier. Though many of them offer a variety of different ways to take a skiing holiday they have been categorised according to their main strength.

mainstream

airtours t 0870 238 7777,
i mytravel.com
crystal t 0870 160 6040,
i crystalski.co.uk
first choice t 0870 754 3477,
i fcski.co.uk
inghams t 0208 780 4433,
i inghams.co.uk
thomson t 0870 606 1470, i thomson-ski.co.uk

ski-specific

lotus supertravel t 027 204 4699,
i supertravel.co.uk
simply ski t 0208 541 2209,
i simplytravel.co.uk
ski activity t 01738 840 888,
i skiactivity.co.uk
ski club of great britain t 020 8410 2022, i skiclub.co.uk
ski independence t 0870 600 1462,
i ski-independence.co.uk
ski julia t 0138 658 4478,
i skijulia.co.uk
ski world t 0870 241 6723,
i skiworld.ltd.uk
total ski t 08701 633 633, i skitotal.com

resort-specific

peak ski t 01442 832 629,
i peak-ski.co.uk
ski armadillo t 07781 411 820/07885 187 293, i skiarmadillo.com
ski verbier t 0207 385 8050
i skiverbier.com
snowlife t 0124 522 1266,
i snowlifechaletholidays.com
sports travel company t 079 584 5490/079 383 0852,
i sportstravelcompany.com
verbier chalets t 020 7835 0635,
i skichaletsverbier.co.uk
vertical reality t 01268 452 337,
i verticalrealityverbier.com

luxury

descent t 0207 384 3854,
i descent.co.uk
elegant resorts t 01244 897 333,
i elegantresorts.co.uk

tailor-made & weekends

alpine weekends t 0208 944 9762,
i alpineweekends.co.uk
flexiski t 0870 909 0754,
i flexiski.com
kaluma t 0870 442 8044,
i kalumatravel.co.uk
made to measure t 0124 353 3333,
i madetomeasureholidays.com
momentum ski t 0207 371 9111,
i momentum.uk.com
ski weekend t 0870 060 0615,
i skiweekend.com
white roc ski weekends t 0207 792 1188, i whiteroc.co.uk

self-catering, b&b & budget

interhome t 020 8891 1294,

tour operators

i interhome.co.uk
into mountains i intomountains.com
mountain beds t 0207 924 2650,
i mountainbeds.co.uk
verbier summits t 027 776 1134,
i verbiersummits.com

self-drive

drive alive t 0114 292 2971, i drive-alive.co.uk
erna low t 0207 584 2841,
i ernalow.co.uk

independents

powderwhite i powderwhite.co.uk
snowfalling t 01892 725 379,
i snowfalling.co.uk
the powder co t 07771 850 609,
i thepowderco.com
verbier chalet t 00 41 27 771 9630,
i verbierchalet.com

le châble

chill inn t 0041 788 348033,
i chillinnverbier.com

If you run a ski company that offers holidays to Verbier but are not listed here, let us know by email to comments@snowmole.com and we will include you in the next edition of this guide.

directory

listings

All 027, 024 and 022 numbers need the Swiss international prefix (0041) if dialled from the UK.

transport

air

bmibaby t 0870 264 2229,
i bmibaby.com
british airways t 0870 850 9850,
i ba.com
easyjet t 0870 600 0000, i easyjet.co.uk
swiss t 0845 601 0956 i swiss.com
geneva t 022 717 7111, i gva.ch
sion t 027 329 0600, i sionairport.ch

car hire

alamo i alamo.com
avis i avis.com, t 027 771 3666 (verbier)
easycar t 0906 333 3333, i easycar.com
europcar i europcar.com
hertz t 0870 844 8844 i hertz.co.uk,
t/f 027 771 4553/6362 (verbier)

coach

alpine express t/f 027 771 9600/9601,
i alpinexpress.ch
lemania t 027 771 29 55/027 722 5614

cross-channel

eurotunnel t 0870 535 3535,
i eurotunnel.com
norfolkline t 01304 218400,
i norfolkline.com
speedferries t 01304 203000
i speedferries.com

driving

general - carry a valid driver's licence, proof of ownership, your insurance certificate and an emergency triangle.
petrol - petrol stations are rarely open

at night, but most have automatic distributors, which accept credit cards or cash. Instructions are rarely in English so they can be confusing to use. Verbier has 2 petrol stations - 1 on Rue de Verbier and 1 on Rue de Centre Sportif.
road information - i viamichelin.com, t 163, 24/7 road assistance t 140
signs & rules - motorway signs are green and you need a vignette (a windscreen sticker) to travel on them - buy one at the border. They last for the year in which bought and cost CHF40. You must wear a seatbelt in the front and back of a car. Children under 12 must sit in the back and babies and young children must be placed in special baby/young child seats. Important rules for driving in the mountains are that ascending vehicles have priority and postal buses and pedestrians always have right of way. A handbook on road signs and regulations is available in English from the cantonale police.
speed limits - in villages and suburbs the speed limit is 50km/h (unless indicated). The limit is 80km/h on all other roads and 120km/h on motorways.

helicopter
air glaciers t 027 329 1415
i air-glaciers.ch

international train
raileurope t 0870 584 8848
i raileurope.co.uk
eurostar t 0870 518 6186
i eurostar.com
TGV i tgv.com

local bus
post bus t 027 771 1044
i carpostal.ch

local train
rail service t 0900 300 300,
i railaway.ch, cff.ch
le châble t 027 776 1366
martigny t 027 722 4858

maps
The tourist office has A4-sized maps of the village. OS maps (1:50000 or 1:25000) of the surrounding area are available from the Naville on the Place Centrale.

private minibus
alp line t 0033 677 865282, i alp-line.com
alpine cab i alpinecab.com.
ats t 0709 209 7392, i a-t-s.net
mountain transfers t 07889 942786,
i mountaintransfers.com

health & safety

accidents

If you have an accident on the slopes, you will be taken to the nearest doctor unless you specify a particular one. To confirm you can pay for treatment carry a credit card and your insurance details. At some point, contact your insurance company to check whether they want to arrange your transport home. And ask your doctor for a medical certificate confirming you are fit to travel.
If you see an accident on the slopes, tell the nearest rescue centre, normally at the top or bottom of lifts.

doctors

All of the medical centres are open Mondays-Fridays 8:30am-12pm and 2pm-6pm and Saturday mornings - Cabinet Medical des Arcades (t 027 771 7020/for emergencies 079 447 2572) underneath Migros, Cabinet Medical Square Poste (t 027 771 7001) off Rue de la Poste and Polyclinique Verbier (c3) (t 027 771 6677) on Route des Creux. The medical centres operate an on-call rota (which is displayed in the tourist office) at night, on Sundays and bank holidays. The nearest hospital is in Martigny (t 027 603 9000).

emergency numbers

police t 117
ambulance t 144
fire brigade t 118
24/7 road assistance t 140
bloodwagon t 027 775 2511
air ambulance t 1414
air glaciers t 1415
euro emergency t 112
on-call dentist t 079 606 0550
on-call pharmacy t 0900 558 143
From a phone box, emergency calls are not always free so you may need some change to make the call.

health

UK visitors don't need any vaccinations to enter Switzerland. There isn't a national health service, so you pay for treatment when you receive it.

insurance

Personal insurance covering wintersports and the cost of any ambulances, helicopter rescue and emergency repatriation is essential as all these services are expensive. Insurance policies differ greatly - some exclude off-piste skiing or cover it only if you go with a guide, so check the terms and conditions carefully. Also ensure that après-ski activities, such as tobogganing, are covered. If you do not have any cover before you arrive in Verbier you can buy an Air Glaciers card for CHF30 from any of TéléVerbier's offices.

pharmacies

Pharmacie Internationale (t 027 771 6622) on Rue de Médran and Pharmacie de Verbier (t 027 771 2330) on Route des Creux open Mondays-Saturdays 8:30am-12:30pm and 2:30pm-7pm and Sundays 10am-12:30pm and 3pm-7pm.

physiotherapists

D. Blanjean & M. C. Blanjean-Demilt
t 027 771 82 80

police

Police Cantonale (all crimes) (t 027 775 63 20) on Chemin des Vernes opens Tuesdays, Thursdays and Saturdays 4:30pm-6pm.
Police Municipale (t 027 775 3545) on Rue de Centre Sportif opens 9:30am-12:15pm and 3pm-6:30pm.

safety on the mountain

avalanche danger - the risk of avalanche is graded from 1 to 5.
1. (green) low, generally risk-free conditions.
2. (yellow) moderate, favourable conditions for the most part.
3. (dark yellow) considerable, partly infavourable conditions.
4. (orange) high, partly infavourable conditions.
5. (red) very high, skiing not advised.

TéléVerbier displays the risk each day at the main lift stations, but if you are in any doubt about where it is safe to ski ask their advice.

food & drink - a skiing holiday is not the time to start a diet. Your body expends energy keeping warm and exercising so it's a good idea to eat a decent breakfast, and carry some chocolate or sweets with you.
The body dehydrates more quickly at altitude and whilst exercising. You need to drink lots of water each day to replace the moisture you lose.

rules of conduct - the International Ski Federation publishes conduct rules for all skiers and boarders, as summarised.
1. respect - do not endanger or prejudice the safety of others.
2. control - ski in control, adapting speed and manner to ability, the conditions and the traffic.
3. choice of route - the uphill skier must choose his route so he does not endanger skiers ahead.
4. overtaking - allowed above or below, right or left, but leave enough room for the overtaken skier.
5. entering & starting a run - look up and down the piste when doing so.
6. stopping on the piste - avoid stopping in narrow places or where visibility is restricted.
7. climbing - keep to the side of the piste when climbing up or down.
8. signs & markings - respect these.
9. assistance - every skier must assist at accidents.
10. identification - all involved in an accident (including witnesses) must exchange details.

weather information

Weather and temperature can change quickly in the mountains. A day which starts off as clear and sunny can end in a whirling blizzard. Even in the resort, air temperature can be very low and the higher you go up the mountain, the colder it gets. A strong wind also lowers the overall temperature considerably.
Rhone FM 103.3 broadcasts snow

conditions, the weather forecast, and status of the pistes between 7:30am and 10:30am in English or log onto meteosuisse.ch. Snow and avalanche forecasts can be obtained from Infoneige (t 027 775 2525) or online at slf.ch

what to wear

Several, thin layers are better than one thick piece. Avoid cotton, which keeps moisture next to the body, so cooling it down. A strong and wind and moisture resistant material such as Goretex is best for outer layers. Gloves and a hat are also essential.

Always wear sunglasses (or goggles when cloudy), preferably wrap-around with shatter-proof lenses giving 100% protection from UVA and UVB rays. No or poor eye protection can cause snowblindness - the eyes water and feel painful and gritty. Treat by resting eyes in a darkened room, and applying cold compresses.

The sun is more intense at high altitude, so re-apply a high factor SPF sun protection (from UVA and UVB rays) regularly, even if overcast and cloudy and particularly after falling or sweating. Don't forget ear lobes, and the underside of the nose.

resort survival

army

100 or so UK squaddies and officers stay for 6 weeks from early December for ski training and racing. They can make their presence felt around the resort, but you soon get to know - and avoid - the venues they favour.

banks & ATMs

Banque Cantonale du Valais and UBS on the Place Centrale, Banque Edouard Constant on Rue de la Poste and Credit Suisse on Rue de Verbier open Mondays-Fridays 9am-12pm and 3pm-6pm. All have 24 hour ATMs, which often run out of money at weekends.

church services

The Catholic church holds services in French at 6pm on Saturdays and 11:30am and 6pm on Sundays. A Protestant service in English is held in the Swiss Reformed church at 6pm on Sundays. At 2:30pm on Wednesdays in good weather a *priere du skieur* is held in La Chaux.

internet/email

Harold's hamburgers has 5 iMacs for word processing or internet access and wifi. Open 10am-1:30am, non-members pay CHF1 to log-in and then 30 cents a minute, and members pay 50 cents to log-in (after an initial payment of CHF30) and then 20 cents a minute. Elsewhere, the Pub Mont Fort has a metered terminal in a small alcove off the main pub, whilst the Verbier Beach restaurant in the Centre Sportif has 2 terminals and the Wonderbar has 4. Most phone boxes also have an internet/email facility.

laundry & dry cleaning

Les Arcades by Migros, Charmarel on Rue de Médran and Mirella on Route des Creux all offer laundry and dry cleaning services.

left luggage

You can leave your luggage at the post office on Rue de la Poste.

library

Open (t 027 771 1101) 4pm-6pm on Wednesdays and Fridays and 10am-12pm on Saturdays, 20% of the books are in English. All visitors can obtain temporary membership.

newspapers

English newspapers (and others) - often for the same day - are available from the Naville on the Place Centrale and the small kiosk next to the post office. Expect to pay three times what you would pay in the UK.

parking

Parking along the roads is only allowed where indicated and the police will give you a ticket if you are illegally parked. For long term parking there is a pay & display at Médran 8am-4pm (270 spaces), the Place Centrale 8am-8pm (127 spaces) and the Savoleyres lift station (70 spaces). The Centre Sportif (500 places) has free long-term parking as does Carrefour (15 places) and Les Esserts (60 places) - though cars cannot be left here overnight as snow clearing operations take place. Short term pay & display parking is available on Route des Creux (18 places). There is also free short term parking underneath Migros, next to Coop and by the arcade of shops on Rue de Médran - though all of these spaces are officially for clients of the commerces.

passport photos

There are 2 coin-operated booths at Médran.

post

The post office (t 027 771 1044) on Rue de la Poste opens Mondays-Fridays 8am-12pm and 2pm-6pm and Saturdays 8am-11am. There is a 24 hour stamp machine outside.

shopping

Most shops open every day (except public holidays) 8:30am-12:30am, and 3pm-7pm.

supermarkets - there are 6 - Primo, Coop, Migros, PAM, Denner and the Laterie. Migros only stocks own-brands and does not sell alcohol. Primo on the Place Centrale is the most centrally located but the most expensive. Denner on Rue de Verbier and PAM next to Migros are discount shops so bulk goods or alcohol can be cheaper, whilst the Laterie on Route des Creux is more like a corner shop. On Sundays and some bank holidays, either Primo and Coop or Migros and PAM open - dates and times are posted in their windows.

bread - Michellod has 4 outlets in the resort, 2 of which open at 7:30am to sell fresh bread, pastries, sandwiches, tarts and cakes, as does the bakery on Rue de Verbier.

cheese - La Chaumière on Rue de Médran stocks a mouth-watering selection of international and local cheeses, cured meats and wine. Primo and Migros have cheese counters and all the supermarkets sell pre-packed cheese.

chocolate - all the supermarkets (except Migros) newsagents and newsstands sell the popular Swiss makes - Milka, Lindt, Toblerone. Macbirch sells individually priced chocolates.

fish - you can buy some fish from Primo, Coop and Migros. Le Vivier next to Primo, sells a wider range of fresh and smoked fish as well as some wine and deli products.

meat - Chez Camille, Del Maître and Bruchez Frères all stock a variety of meats and you can also buy rôtisserie chickens - but reserve one in peak weeks - and order a turkey for Christmas. Migros, Primo and Coop have meat counters.

wine & beer - Macbirch (t/f 027 771 4442) has 2 outlets - one on Rue de Verbier and the other on Rue de Médran - both of which stock local and global wines and spirits and will deliver for

free. All the supermarkets, except Migros, sell wine, beer and spirits.
children - L'Igloo and Le Mode des Montagnes for outdoor and indoor clothing and Cartoon and Toy's World for toys and games.
clothes - Week End and Degagee for designer labels, Patagonia and Quiksilver for outdoor wear and Soie Coquine for ladies lingerie and swimwear. All of these shops are on Rue de Médran.
florists - Gailland (t 027 771 1717) on Rue de Verbier sells beautiful floral arrangements and will deliver.
gifts - Swiss Souvenirs does what it says on the tin selling cuckoo clocks, stuffed St. Bernard dogs and Swiss Army knifes. BRV, L'Atelier d'Elo and Yves Jacot sell a selection of watches and jewellery.

ski equipment storage

Lockers are located at Médran - CHF2 for a small locker or ski holder and CHF5 for a big locker. The locker takes your coin as soon as you shut the door, so make sure you have put in/taken out everything you need.

taxis

The tourist office has a full list of taxis in Verbier. The ones below speak decent English.
Michaud Pascal t 027 771 7196/ 078 721 2121
Pierrette Coquoz t 027 771 1843/ 079 606 0966 - friendly and reliable
Fernades Fransisco t 027 771 3465/ 079 220 2088.

tourist information

The tourist office (t/f 027 775 3888/3889, i verbier.ch) on the Place Centrale opens Mondays-Fridays 8:30am-12:30pm and 2pm-6:30pm, Saturdays 8:30pm-7pm and Sundays 9am-12pm and 4pm-6:30pm. Most information is free and available in English.

tv, video & dvd

Swisscom on Rue de la Poste rents TVs, video and DVD players, video-tapes and DVDs while Contact Immobilier & Video club 7/7 on Rue de Verbier rents DVDs and Videotapes.

wcs

There are public loos at Médran, Savoleyres and Les Ruinettes.

websites

One of the best is verbinet.com - information includes accommodation and events listings and snow, weather and road reports. The official tourist office website (i verbier.ch) is also very informative.

country survival

customs
UK visitors over 17 can take 200 cigarettes, 50 cigars or 250g of pipe tobacco, 1 litre of alcohol over 15% proof, 2 litres of alcohol below 15% proof and gifts up to the value of CHF100 out of Switzerland.

electricity
220 volts/50hz ac. Appliances use a two-pin plug - you can buy adaptors at Geneva airport or in Verbier at the Swisscom shop on Rue de la Poste.

language
Verbier is in French-speaking Switzerland, though information is also displayed in Swiss-German and Italian. English is widely spoken.

money
The currency is the Swiss Franc (SFr/CHF) - CHF1 is 100 centimes. Notes come in CHF10, 20, 50, 100, 200, 1,000 and coins in CHF1, 2, 5 and cents 5, 10, 20, 50. In 2004 the average exchange rate for UK£1 was CHF2.2. Some places also accept Euros. You can exchange money in all the banks in Verbier during the week and also at the airport and train stations. You can change money at the tourist office, TéléVerbier or the 'Bazar' at the Vallée Blanche on Rue de Médran at weekends. You can change CHF notes for CHF coins at the change machine at Médran.

passports & visas
UK citizens don't need a visa but your passport should have at least 6 months until expiry. UK visitors can stay for 3 months (although passports are rarely stamped) - and you need a work permit for a longer stay (➡ seasonnaires). All Swiss citizens must carry personal ID, so it's a good idea to carry your passport with you.

public holidays
December 6 - St Nicholas Day
25 - Christmas Day
26 - St Stephen's day
January 1 - New Year's Day
March 19 - St Joseph's day
March/April Good Friday, Easter Sunday & Monday

telephone
Phones boxes are located by and opposite the post office in Verbier. The minimum cost of any call is 60ct and you can pay by phone card (CHF5/10/20 sold at the post office, and train and petrol stations), credit card or a Swisscom International Prepaid Card (CHF 10/20/50/100). All local and most international calls are cheaper 5pm-8am. The international dialling code for Switzerland is 0041; the free international operator 0800 801 141; international direct enquiries 1159; and national direct enquiries 111. Swisscom, Sunrise and Orange are the mobile phone networks.

time
Switzerland is always 1 hour ahead of England.

tipping
Restaurants are obliged by law to work a service charge into the bill, so you don't need to leave an additional tip unless you want to.

UK embassy & consulates
UK embassy - Bern t 0313 597 700
Consulate - Geneva t 0227 981 605

water
Tap water is drinkable, except where there is a eau non potable sign.

glossary

a

arête - a sharp ridge.

avalanche - a rapid slide of snow down a slope.

avalanche transceiver - a device used when skiing off-piste, which can both emit and track a high frequency signal to allow skiers lost in an avalanche or a crevasse to be found.

b

BASI - British Association of Snowsport Instructors.

binding - attaches boot to ski.

black run/piste - difficult, generally steeper than a red piste.

blood wagon - a stretcher on runners used by ski patrollers to carry injured skiers off the mountain.

blue run/piste - easy, generally wide with a gentle slope.

bubble ➡ 'gondola'.

button (or Poma) lift - for 1 person. Skis and boards run along the ground, whilst you sit on a small 'button' shaped seat.

c

cable car - a large box-shaped lift, running on a thick cable over pylons high above the ground, which carry up to 250 people per car.

carving - a recently developed turning technique used by skiers and boarders to make big, sweeping turns across the piste.

carving skis - shorter and fatter than traditional skis, used for carving turns.

chairlift - like a small and uncomfortable sofa, which scoops you and your skis off the ground and carries you up the mountain. Once on, a protective bar with a rest for your skis holds you in place. Can carry 2-6 people.

couloir - a 'corridor' between 2 ridges, normally steep and narrow.

crampons - spiked fittings attached to outdoor or ski boots to climb mountains or walk on ice.

d

draglift or (T-bar) - for 2 people. Skis and boards run on the ground, whilst you lean against a small bar.

drop-off - a sharp increase in gradient.

e

edge - the metal ridge on the border of each side of the ski.

f

FIS - Federation Internationale du Ski.

flat light - lack of contrast caused by shadow or cloud, making it very difficult to judge depth and distance.

freeriding, freeskiing - off-piste skiing.

freestyle - skiing involving jumps.

g

glacier - a slow-moving ice mass formed thousands of years ago and fed each year by fresh snow.

gondola (or bubble) - an enclosed lift, often with seats.

h

heliskiing - off-piste skiing on routes only accessible by helicopter.

high mountain tour (orange) - not groomed, maintained or patrolled. Should be skied with a guide.

high season - weeks when the resort is (generally) at full capacity.

glossary

i

itinerary route (yellow) - not groomed, maintained or patrolled. Generally more difficult than a black piste. Can be skied without a guide.

k

kicker - jump.

l

lambchop drag ➥ 'rope tow'.

ledgy - off-piste conditions in which there are many short, sharp drop-offs.

low season - beginning and end of the season and the least popular weeks in mid-January.

m

mid season - reasonably popular weeks in which the resort is busy but not full.

mogul - a bump, small or large, on or off piste. A large mogulled area is called a mogul field.

o

off-piste - the area away from marked, prepared and patrolled pistes.

p

parallel turn - skis turn in parallel.

piste - a ski run marked, groomed and patrolled, and graded in terms of difficulty (blue, red or black).

piste basher - a bulldozer designed to groom pistes by smoothing snow.

pisteur - a ski piste patroller.

Poma ➥ 'button lift'.

powder - fresh, unbashed or untracked snow.

r

raquettes ➥ 'snowshoes'.

red run/piste - intermediate, normally steeper than a blue piste, although a flatish piste may be a red because it is narrow, has a steep drop-off or because snow conditions are worse than on other pistes.

rope tow (or lambchop drag) - a constantly moving loop of rope with small handles to grab onto to take you up a slope.

s

schuss - a straight slope down which you can ski very fast.

seasonnaire - an individual who lives (and usually works) in a ski resort for the season.

skis - technology has changed in the last 10 years. New skis are now shorter and wider. When renting, you will be given a pair approx. 5-10cms shorter than your height.

ski patrol - a team of piste patrollers

skins - artificial fur attached to ski base, for ski touring.

snow-chains - chains attached to car tyres so that it can be driven (cautiously) over snow or ice.

snowshoes - footwear resembling tennis rackets which attach to shoes, for walking on soft snow.

spring snow - granular, heavy snow conditions common in late season (when daytime temperatures rise causing snow to thaw and re-freeze).

steeps - a slope with a very steep gradient.

t

T-bar ➥ 'draglift'.

w

white-out - complete lack of visibility caused by enveloping cloud cover.

index

index

also available...

the snowmole guides to

chamonix mont-blanc
including argentière and full coverage of chamonix's 4 ski areas and the vallée blanche...

courchevel les 3 vallées
including 1850, 1650, 1550, le praz & la tania and full coverage of the 3 vallées ski area ...

la plagne paradiski
including all 10 resorts and full coverage of the paradiski area and the vanoise express...

les arcs paradiski
including peisey-vallandry & arc 1950 and full coverage of the paradiski area and the vanoise express...

also available...

méribel les 3 vallées
including méribel centre, les allues, méribel village & mottaret and full coverage of the 3 vallées ski area...

val d'isère espace killy
including st. foy and full coverage of the espace killy area...

zermatt matterhorn
including full coverage of the zermatt-cervinia ski area and the matterhorn

and coming soon the snowmole guides to...

st. anton arlberg
tignes espace killy
ski weekends
alpine secrets

& also the underground network

further information

accuracy & updates

We have tried our best to ensure that all the information included is accurate at the date of publication. However, because places change - improve, get worse, or even close - you may find things different when you get there. Also, everybody's experience is different and you may not agree with our opinion. You can help us, in 2 ways: by letting us know of any changes you notice and by telling us what you think - good or bad - about what we've written. If you have any comments, ideas or suggestions, please write to us at: snowmole, 45 Mysore Road, London, SW11 5RY or send an email to comments@snowmole.com

snowmole.com

Our website is intended as a compliment to our guides. Constantly evolving and frequently updated with news, you will find links to other wintersport related websites, information on our stockists and offers and the latest news about future editions and new titles. We also use our website to let you know of any major changes that occur after we publish the guides.

If you would like to receive news and updates about our books by email, please register your details at www.snowmole.com

order form

The snowmole guides are available from all major bookshops, wintersports retailers or direct from Qanuk Publishing & Design Ltd. To experience the Alps without leaving home have your next snowmole guide delivered to your door. To order send an email to sales@snowmole.com or fill in the form below and send it to us at Qanuk Publishing & Design Ltd, 45 Mysore Road, London, SW11 5RY

the snowmole guide to:	ISBN	quantity
chamonix mont blanc	0-9545739-3-5	--------------------------
courchevel les 3 vallées	0-9545739-5-1	--------------------------
la plagne paradiski	0-9545739-8-6	--------------------------
les arcs paradiski	0-9545739-7-8	--------------------------
méribel les 3 vallées	0-9545739-4-3	--------------------------
val d'isère espace killy	0-9545739-9-4	--------------------------
verbier val de bagnes	0-9545739-2-7	--------------------------
zermatt matterhorn	0-9545739-6-X	--------------------------

total: --------------------------
(£6.99 each, postage & packaging free)

I enclose a cheque for £
(made payable to Qanuk Publishing & Design Ltd)

name --
address --
postcode --
tel --
email address --
(please use block capitals)

Delivery will normally be within 14 working days. The availability and published prices quoted are correct at the time of going to press but are subject to alteration without prior notice. Please note that this service is only available in the UK.

Qanuk would like to keep you updated on new titles in the snowmole range or special offers. If you do not wish to receive such information please tick here ☐
Qanuk has a number of partners in the ski industry, and we may from time to time share your details with those partners if we think it might be of interest to you. If you do not wish us to share your details please tick here ☐

about you

Your comments, opinions and recommendations are very important to us. To help us improve the snowmole guides, please take a few minutes to complete this short questionnaire. Once completed please send it to us at Qanuk Publishing & Design Ltd.

name (Mr/Mrs/Ms) --
address --
postcode --
email address --
age --
occupation --

1. about your ski holiday (circle as appropriate)
how many days do you ski each year?
weekend/1 week/2 weeks/1 month/more
when do you book?
last-minute/1 month before/1-3 months before/3-6 months before/6+ months before
how do you book your holiday?
travel agent/mainstream tour operator/ski-specific tour operator/diy

2. about the snowmole guide
which title did you buy? --
where and when did you buy it? --
have you bought any other snowmole guides? --
if so, which one(s) --
how would you rate each section out of 5 (1 = useless, 5 = very useful)
getting started --
the skiing --
the resort --
the directory --
the maps --
what in particular made you buy this guide? --
----
do you have any general comments or suggestions? --
----
did you buy any other guides for your holiday? --
if yes, which one? --
Qanuk Publishing & Design Ltd may use information about you to provide you with details of other products and services, by telephone, email or in writing. If you do not wish to receive such details please tick here ☐

lac des vaux, attelas & la chaux

lift		time	pistes & routes				queues		moguls I	moguls II	moguls III	off-piste I	off-piste II	off-piste III
funispace	30	6m55	■	■	■		🚶🚶	!	●	●			●	●
attelas 2	4	7m30	■	■			🚶		●			●		
attelas 3	2	7m30	■	■					●			●		
la combe 2	2	6m55		■						●			●	
fontenay	2	7m20	■	■		■				●	●		●	●
mont gelé	60	8m00				■				●	●		●	●
lac des vaux 1	4	2m25	■	■	■		🚶🚶	!	●	●		●	●	●
lac des vaux 3	3	6m20		■		■	🚶			●	●		●	●
la chaux 1	2	7m25	■	■			🚶🚶🚶	!	●	●				
la chaux 2	4	8m00	■	■			🚶🚶	!				●		

i	
mont gelé	often closed in high winds
lac des vaux 1	alternative route back to verbier if there is a backlog at chassoure tortin
la chaux 2	ski schools have priority on this lift making it a slow journey
fontenay	snowpark access
la chaux 1	snowpark access

lac des vaux,attelas & la chaux

1	attelas
2	l'olympique
3	la chaux
4	cabane du mont fort
5	kiosk
6	ruinettes

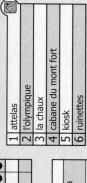

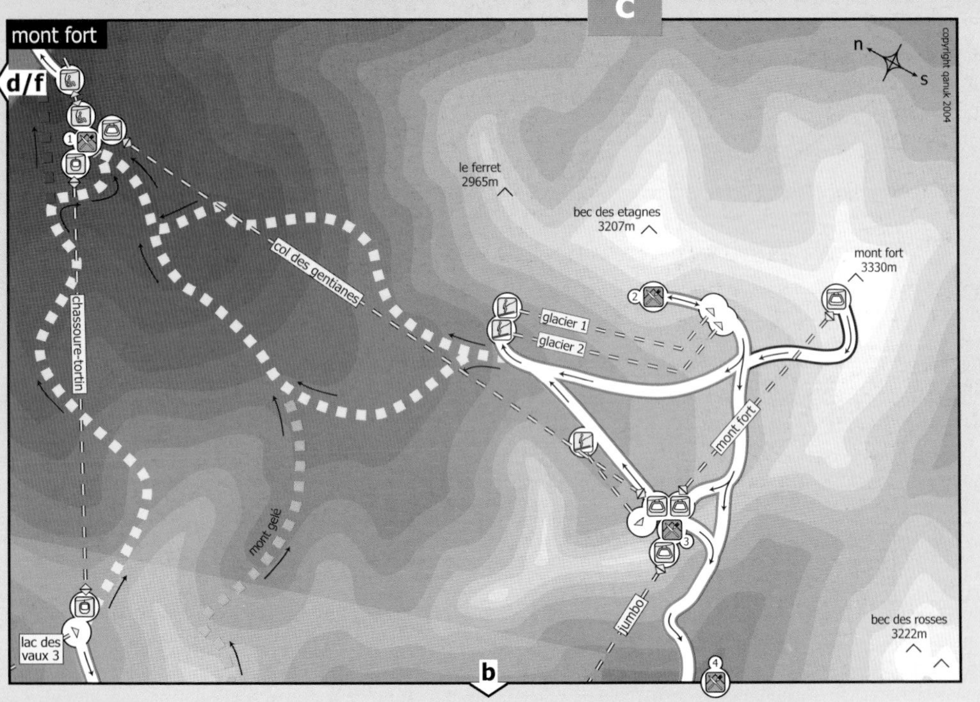
mont fort
d/f
copyright qanuk 2004
n
s
le ferret
2965m
bec des etagnes
3207m
mont fort
3330m
col des gentianes
chassoure-tortin
glacier 1
glacier 2
mont fort
mont gelé
jumbo
lac des
vaux 3
bec des rosses
3222m
b
1
2
3
4

mont fort

lift		⏱	pistes & routes				queues		moguls I	moguls II	moguls III	off-piste I	off-piste II	off-piste III
mont fort	100	4m10			■		queue	!		●	●		●	●
i jumbo	150	6m05		■		■	queue		●	●		●	●	
glacier 1/2	2	6m30		■		■								
i col des gentianes	125	7m35		■		■	queue	!		●	●		●	●
i chassoure-tortin	8	7m45		■		■	queue	!		●	●		●	●

i	
jumbo	take the red piste from the top to reach the cabane du mont fort
chassoure-tortin	you can descend in this lift to reach the 4 vallées without skiing the tortin itinerary
col des gentianes	expect to wait at least 10 minutes between the arrival of the lift and the next departure

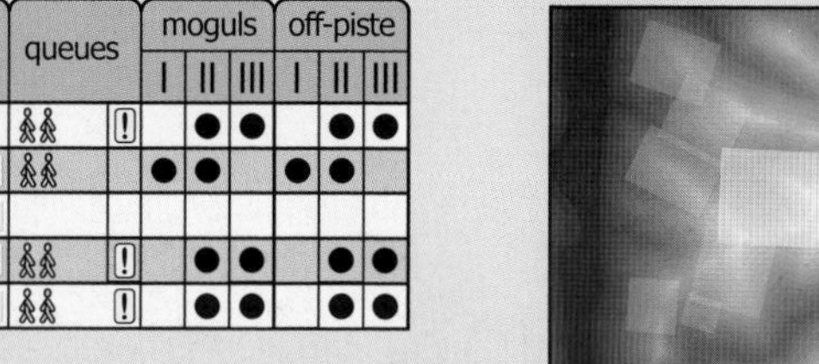

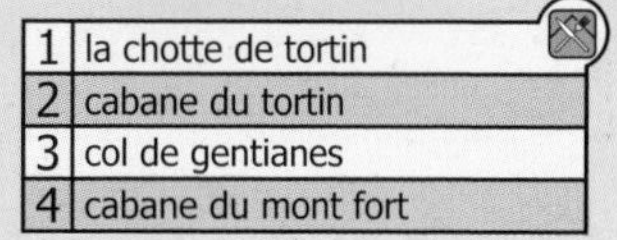

1	la chotte de tortin
2	cabane du tortin
3	col de gentianes
4	cabane du mont fort

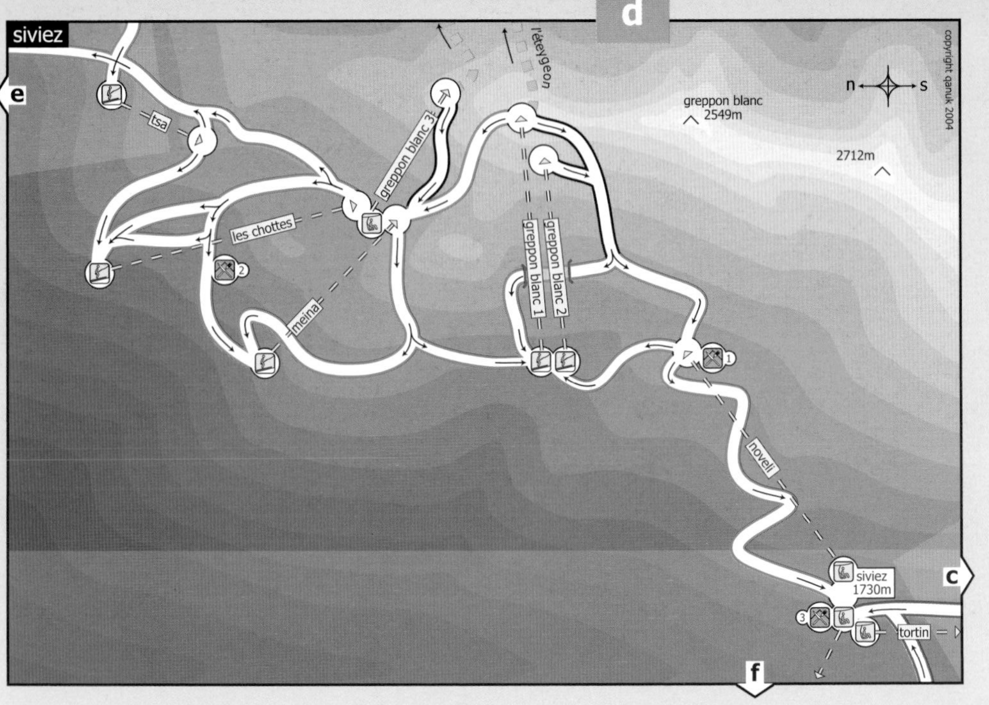
siviez
d
l'éteygeon
copyright qanuk 2004
n
s
greppon blanc
2549m
2712m
e
tsa
greppon blanc 3
les chottes
greppon blanc 1
greppon blanc 2
meina
1
2
3
noveli
siviez
1730m
c
tortin
f

siviez

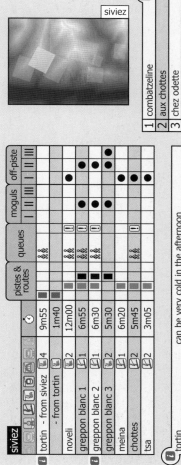

	lifts	time	pistes & routes			queues		moguls I	moguls II	moguls III	off-piste I	off-piste II	off-piste III
tortin - from siviez	4	9m55	■			🚶🚶							
- from tortin		1m40	■										
noveli	2	12m00		■		🚶🚶	(!)				●		
greppon blanc 1	1	6m55		■	■	🚶🚶	(!)		●			●	
greppon blanc 2	1	6m30		■	■	🚶🚶	(!)		●			●	
greppon blanc 3	2	5m30			■				●			●	●
meina	1	6m20		■							●		
chottes	2	5m45		■		🚶🚶	(!)				●		
tsa	2	3m05		■							●		

tortin	can be very cold in the afternoon
greppon blanc 2	when returning to verbier you can get off halfway if you are short of time

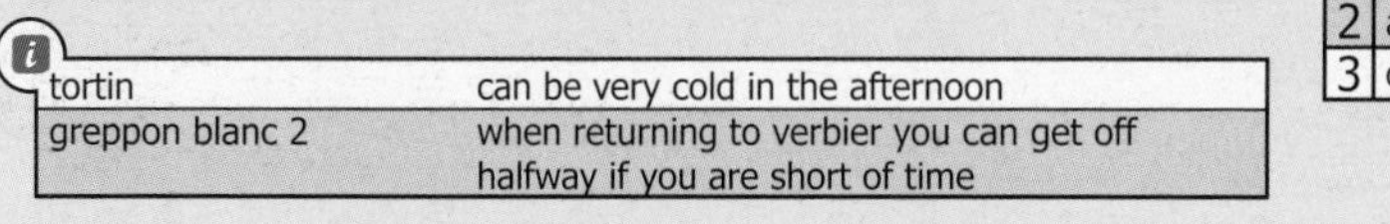
siviez

1	combatzeline
2	aux chottes
3	chez odette

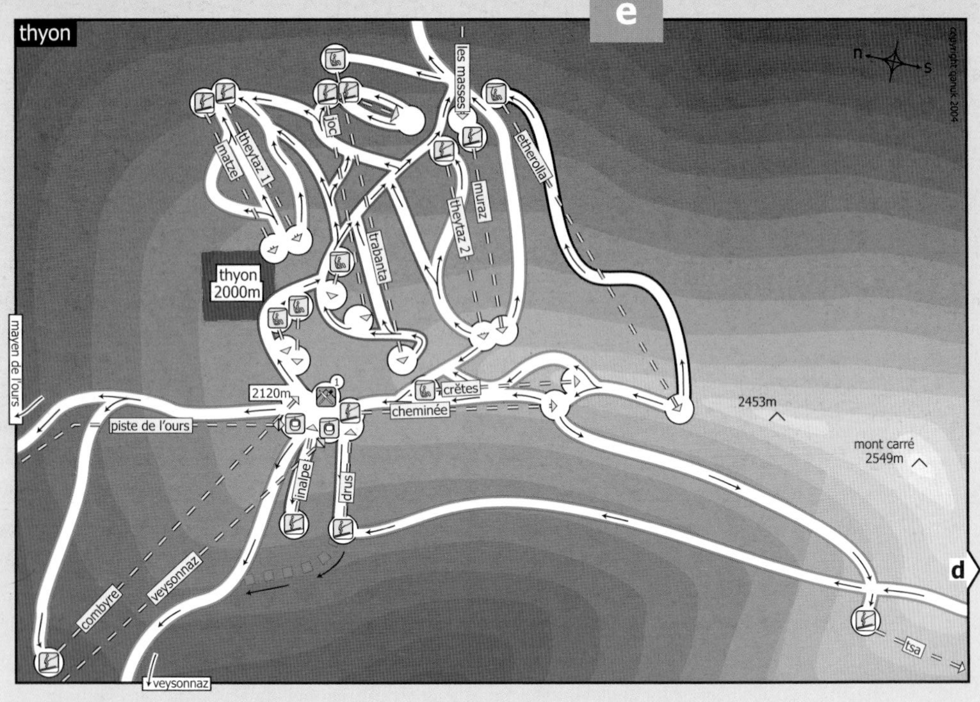

thyon
e
copyright ganuk 2004
n
s
les masses
joc
theytaz 1
matze
muraz
theytaz 2
etherolla
trabanta
thyon
2000m
2120m
1
crêtes
cheminée
piste de l'ours
mayen de l'ours
inalpe
drus
2453m
mont carré
2549m
d
combyre
veysonnaz
veysonnaz
tsa

thyon		⏱	pistes & routes			queues	moguls			off-piste		
							I	II	III	I	II	III
etherolla	2	12m05		■	■							
les masses	2	12m00	■	■						●		
muraz	2	7m30		■						●		
theytaz 2	2	7m20		■						●		
trabanta	4	12m00	■	■						●		
joc	2	7m30	■			🚶				●		
theytaz 1	1	5m20		■						●		
matze	2	5m30		■						●		
les crêtes	2	5m30		■								
cheminée	2	5m15		■								
piste de l'ours	4	9m15	■	■		🚶🚶				●		
combyre	2	6m30	■	■						●		
drus	2	4m00	■	■								
veysonnaz	4	15m00	■	■		🚶🚶				●		

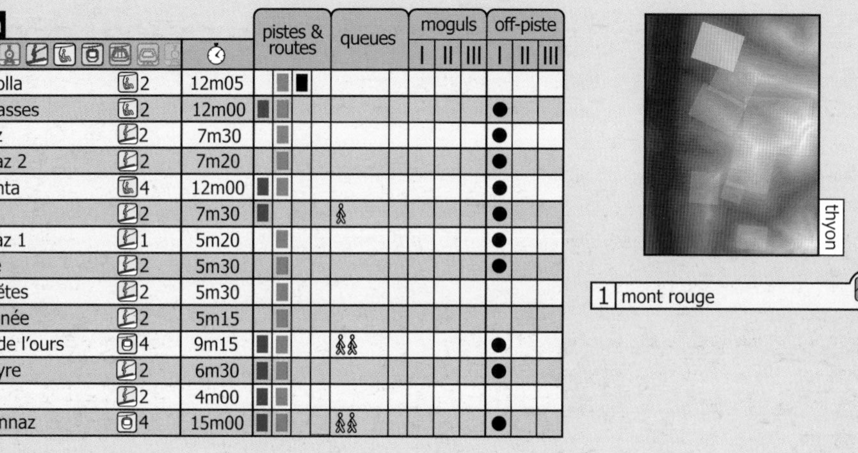

thyon

1 mont rouge

e

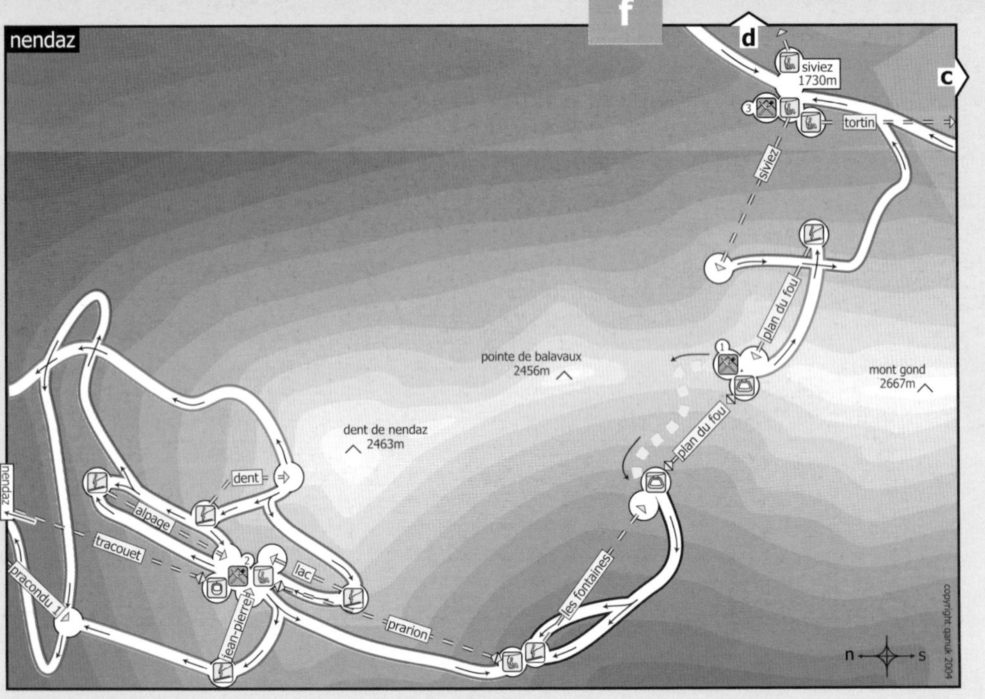
nendaz
d
c
siviez
1730m
3
tortin
siviez
plan du fou
1
pointe de balavaux
2456m
mont gond
2667m
plan du fou
dent de nendaz
2463m
dent
nendaz
alpage
tracouet
2
lac
les fontaines
pracondu 1
jean-pierre
prarion
n
s
copyright qanuk 2004

nendaz			pistes & routes				queues		moguls I	moguls II	moguls III	off-piste I	off-piste II	off-piste III
siviez	2	7m20	■									●		
plan du fou	2	7m00		■		■				●	●		●	●
plan du fou	60	5m30		■		■				●	●		●	●
les fontaines	2	6m00			■									
prarion	4	7m10	■											
jean-pierre	2	5m00	■											
pracondu 1	2	7m30	■											
tracouet	12	12m30	■				🚶🚶							
alpage	2	4m30	■											
dent	1	4m30	■	■										
lac	1	1m00	■											

siviez — when this lift is closed, the only way to access the skiing in nendaz is to take the bus from siviez to nendaz village

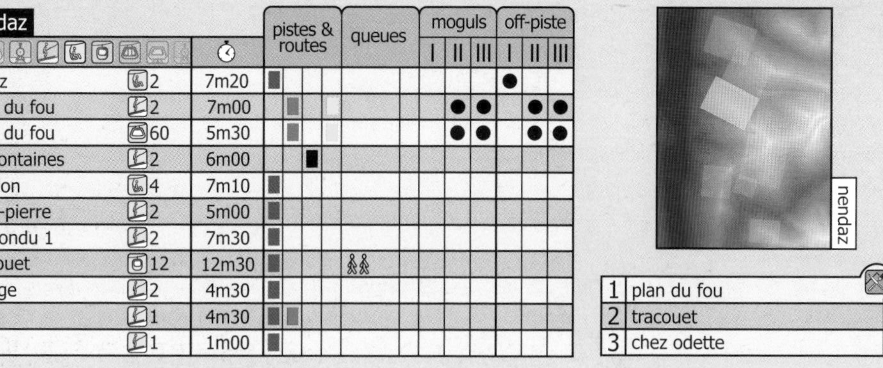

nendaz

1	plan du fou
2	tracouet
3	chez odette

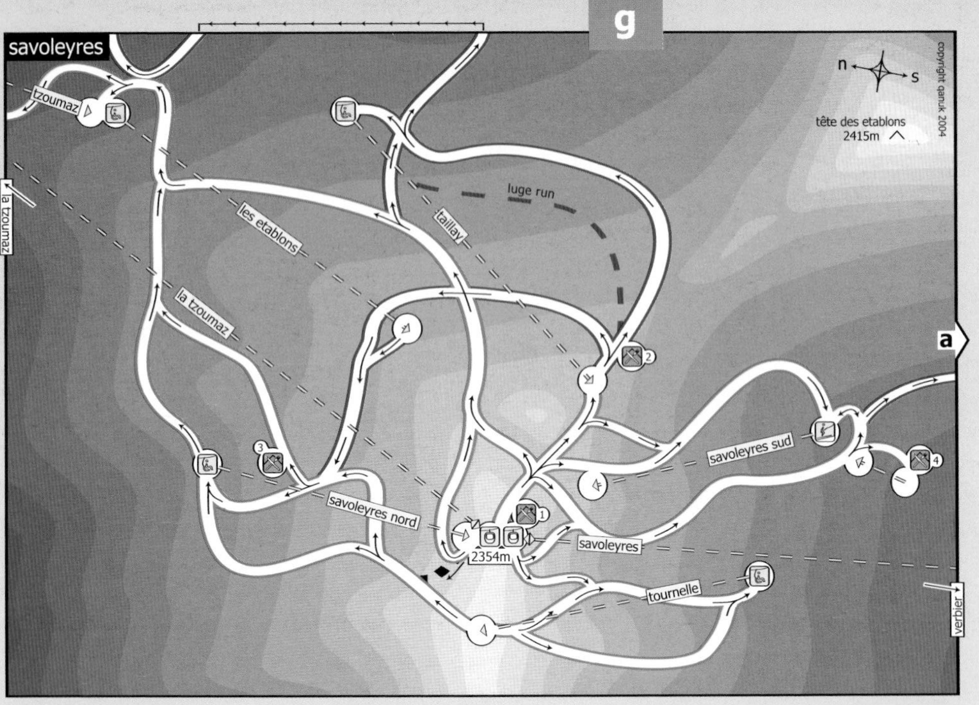
savoleyres
copyright qanuk 2004
n
s
tête des etablons
2415m
luge run
les etablons
taillay
la tzoumaz
tzoumaz
la tzoumaz
savoleyres nord
2354m
savoleyres
savoleyres sud
tournelle
verbier
a
1
2
3
4

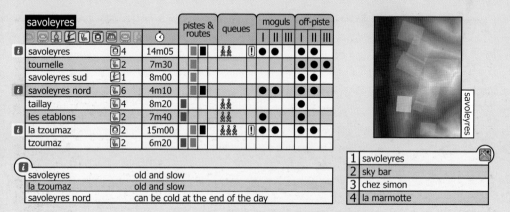

savoleyres	lifts	⏱	pistes & routes				queues		moguls I	moguls II	moguls III	off-piste I	off-piste II	off-piste III
savoleyres	4	14m05		■	■		♟♟	!	●	●		●	●	
tournelle	2	7m30		■								●	●	●
savoleyres sud	1	8m00		■								●	●	
savoleyres nord	6	4m10		■	■				●	●		●	●	
taillay	4	8m20	■				♟♟					●		
les etablons	2	7m40	■				♟♟		●			●		
la tzoumaz	2	15m00		■	■		♟♟♟	!	●	●		●	●	
tzoumaz	2	6m20	■	■										

savoleyres	old and slow
la tzoumaz	old and slow
savoleyres nord	can be cold at the end of the day

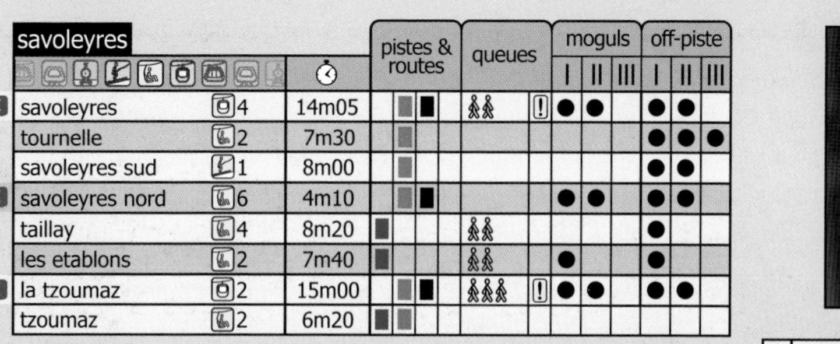
savoleyres

1	savoleyres
2	sky bar
3	chez simon
4	la marmotte

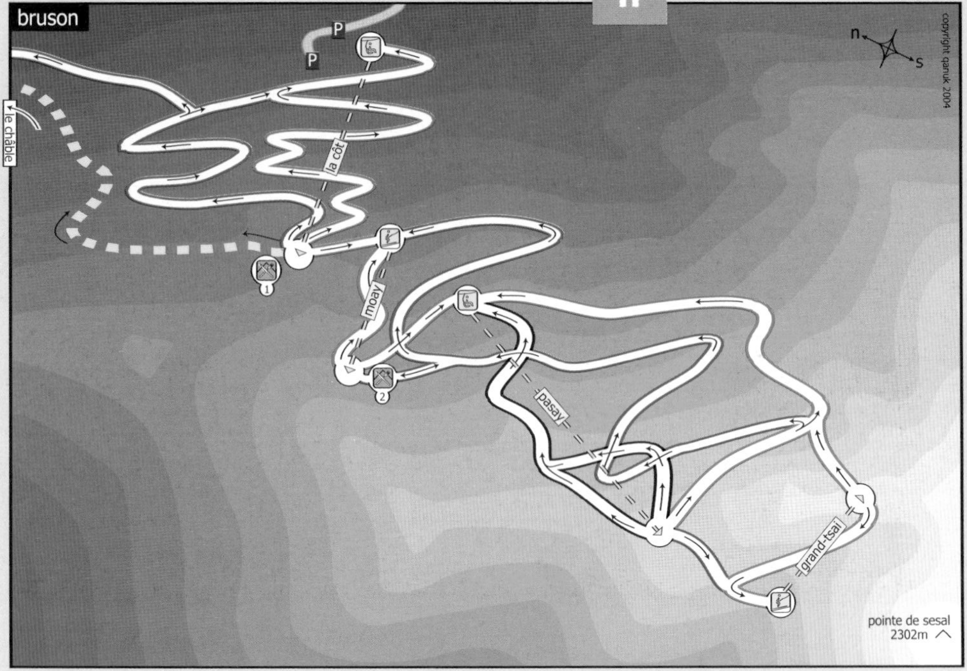

bruson

P
P
le châble
la côt
1
moay
2
pasay
grand-tsai
n
s
pointe de sesal
2302m

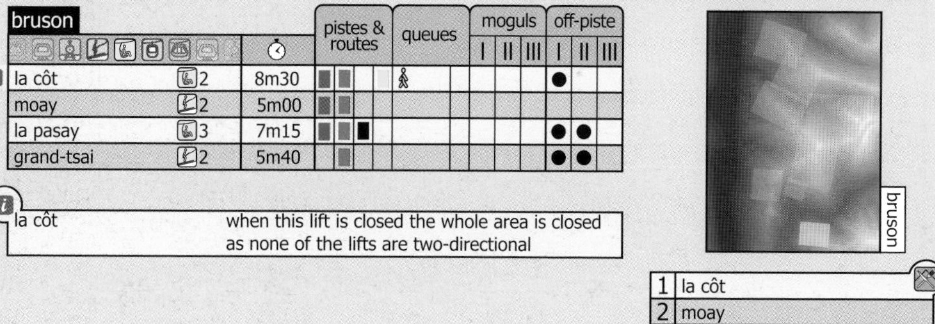

bruson		⏱	pistes & routes	queues	moguls I	moguls II	moguls III	off-piste I	off-piste II	off-piste III
la côt	2	8m30						●		
moay	2	5m00								
la pasay	3	7m15						●	●	
grand-tsai	2	5m40						●	●	

la côt — when this lift is closed the whole area is closed as none of the lifts are two-directional

1	la côt
2	moay

ski area key

a - ruinettes
b - lac des vaux, attelas
& la chaux
c - mont fort
d - siviez
e - thyon
f - nendaz
g - savoleyres
h - bruson

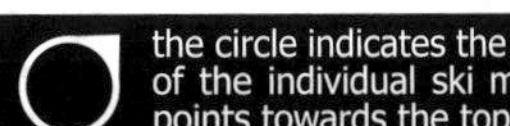

the circle indicates the page orientation of the individual ski maps - the arrow points towards the top of the page